HOW TO WIN FIENDS AND INFLUENCE PEOPLE

BY THE SAME AUTHOR

THE DEVIL'S DIARIES:
THE COLLECTED JOURNALS OF THE DARK LORD

THE RICHEST WHORE IN BABYLON

IF AT FIRST YOU DON'T SUCCEED … CHEAT

**BAD HABITS
AND HOW TO ACQUIRE THEM**

HOW TO WIN FIENDS AND INFLUENCE PEOPLE

666 WICKED WAYS TO GUARANTEE SUCCESS IN THE WORKPLACE

Nicholas D. Satan

AS TRANSCRIBED BY
Professor M.J. Weeks

THE LYONS PRESS
Guilford, Connecticut
An imprint of The Globe Pequot Press

Copyright © The Ivy Press Limited 2009

First Lyons Press edition, 2009

Library of Congress Cataloging-in-Publication Data
is available on file.

ISBN 978-1-59921-568-6

Printed in China

10 9 8 7 6 5 4 3 2 1

This book was conceived, designed, and produced by
Ivy Press
210 High Street
Lewes, East Sussex
BN7 2NS, UK

Creative Director Peter Bridgewater
Publisher Jason Hook
Editorial Director Tom Kitch
Senior Editor Lorraine Turner
Art Director Wayne Blades
Design and Illustration Joerg Hartmannsgruber
Text Marcus Weeks

PICTURE CREDITS
AKG Images: 55. **Corbis**/Bettmann: 91. **Getty Images**:
17T, 20, 65, 111, 115, 125, 134, 147; The Bridgeman Art
Library: 44; John Giustina: 121; Hulton Archive: 105,
129, 143; Karen Moskowitz: 48; Gary Nolton: 102;
Popperfoto: 75, 87; Time & Life Pictures: 71, 101;
Wirelmage: 17B, 40, 151.

This book is dedicated to all the politicians, rulers, business people, lawyers, bankers, and property developers who have come to me for advice. They learned their lessons well, and their achievements show the effectiveness of my guidance. I thank them for their small sacrifices, which have not been in vain.

N.D.S.

SIX THINGS THIS BOOK 666
WILL HELP YOU ACHIEVE

- ➤ More material wealth than you could possibly need

- ➤ The gratification of all your heart's desires

- ➤ The freedom to indulge in a leisurely and enjoyable lifestyle with minimum effort

- ➤ The power to make people do what you want them to do

- ➤ The admiration and envy of all around you

- ➤ Fame, fortune, authority, and influence beyond your wildest dreams

WHAT MORE COULD YOU WANT?

The 666 Principle has worked for me and my countless disciples, so why not make it work for you—what have you got to lose?*

* Other than your eternal soul, that is. Subject to contract.

Normal terms and conditions apply.

CONTENTS

TRIDENT TESTED

HOW THIS BOOK WAS WRITTEN AND WHY

It was my great honor, a few years ago, to edit the journals of Nicholas D. Satan for publication. Working closely with the author's agents, it soon became apparent to all of us how much wisdom and advice the Dark Lord has to offer; among the many papers I was privileged to have access to was a positive cornucopia of notes and jottings, quotes and cuttings, all of which gave some insight into the diabolic philosophy that has proved so successful.

At first, His Satanic Majesty was wary of sharing what he considered to be "trade secrets" in these private papers, but after much sycophantic encouragement was persuaded to impart at least some of his vast knowledge of the principles of self-improvement to a wider public.

Previously, I had only met the Great One at the signing of our original contract (a memorable occasion, marred only by an unfortunate accident involving a paper cut to my finger just before appending my signature), but for this project He insisted on working closely with me to realize a faithful presentation of his vision. Fortuitously, I had been offered a post at a university only a short distance from His earthly offices coincident with the period of our collaboration, facilitating regular meetings and allowing work to progress apace.

**During the course of our many discussions,
several things became obvious:**

➤ That, with a few notable exceptions (the work of Machiavelli and de Sade, for example), self-help books had thus far been woefully misinformed

➤ That we had in front of us a wealth of practical advice based on millennia of successful experience in the art of self-advancement

- That it was possible to organize this to offer a systematic approach to acquiring a range of advantageous life skills

- That those perceptive few who had already approached the Diabolic Master for guidance had without exception achieved their goals

- That the majority of people are unaware of the techniques by which they can enrich their lives

- That people would be eager to invest in an instructive manual imparting such information, and make a body-and-soul commitment to its ideals

This was enough to convince Satan that the time for this book was long overdue, and its publication could prove as successful and popular as His other projects.

I have endeavored to capture the excitement of our discoveries and the enthusiasm of the Devil for all His Works by including where appropriate the original manuscripts and documents, but where this has proved impracticable I have transcribed and edited them under His supervision and with His approval. The Masterstroke—codifying the six principal tenets and their six basic principles in a sixfold, step-by-step program—was the Dark Lord's very own, and credit for all the valuable advice and brilliant analysis contained in this volume is due to Him and Him alone. Any errors, inaccuracies, or oversights are entirely the responsibility of the editor, who humbly craves forgiveness for his shortcomings.

M. J. Weeks

M. J. Weeks

Visiting Professor of Comparative Theological Anthropology and Business Studies

University of South Baghdad

OUCH! Bet that paper cut still smarts!

HOW TO USE THIS BOOK

A step-by-step guide to acquiring the diabolic habits that will put you on the path to Power, Potency, and Position, this book offers both practical advice and in-depth analysis to ensure you realize your dominance potential. By working through the six sections, examining the six Principles at each stage, and critically applying the six guidelines for successful learning outcomes below, you will achieve an accelerating Personal Development Curve, and by the end of the course will have the knowledge and skills to ride roughshod over your rivals.

So, at each step in the book, use the following guidelines:

➤ **R**ecognize your personal qualities

➤ **E**valuate your capacity for achieving

➤ **A**ctivate each lesson learned

➤ **D**evelop strategies for self-improvement

➤ **I**dentify shortcomings and exploit them

➤ **T**est your capabilities

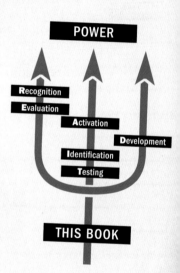

POWER

Recognition
Evaluation
Activation
Development
Identification
Testing

THIS BOOK

THE SIX PRACTICES OF EXCEPTIONALLY POWERFUL PEOPLE

The best way to learn anything is by example, and what better example can there be than those who have made it to the top? Invariably, the exceptionally powerful follow six proven practices. These Six Practices are derived from my own Code of Six Basic Principles: Greed, Lust, Sloth, Wrath, Envy, and Pride—a prescription so successful that rival self-improvement manuals (including what is laughably known as "The Good Book"—ha!) have taken it on board and warn against its winning formula. Strangely, most of these make an unnecessary distinction between Greed and Gluttony, to fit their obsession with the number seven. I can't understand why those so-called self-help gurus are so hung up on numerology.

In brief, follow these proven six Practices of the Powerful and remember to:

➤ **T**ake whatever's there for the taking

➤ **H**unger for the things you want

➤ **R**esist the temptation to exert yourself

➤ **U**nleash your inner demon

➤ **S**eize from anyone who's got what you want

➤ **T**ell the world how great you are

666

TRIDENT TESTED

MISSION STATEMENT

STATEMENT OF VISION

A world where those with the will, courage, and egotism to follow these precepts will achieve the prosperity, influence, and power they deserve.

6 CORE VALUES

➤ Acquisition of all you can get
➤ Ambition to always go that extra mile
➤ Abdication of all responsibility
➤ Aggression against all obstacles
➤ Appropriation of property, funds, and ideas—no matter whose
➤ Aggrandizement of your achievements

6 STRATEGIC PRIORITIES

➤ To harness the energy of insatiability
➤ To appropriately channel the force of desire
➤ To minimize exhaustion caused by unnecessary exertion
➤ To assertively remove the obstacles to achievement
➤ To reverse the negativity of deprivation by transfer of assets
➤ To publicize the efficacy of these principles

6 KEY PERFORMANCE INDICATORS

➤ A healthy bank balance
➤ A healthy sex life
➤ A healthy work to leisure ratio—ideally 1:100
➤ A healthy social circle—enemies, not rivals; collaborators, not friends
➤ A healthy number of underlings, and no significant superiors
➤ A healthy coverage of your exploits in the media

Nicholas D. Satan

Nicholas D. Satan
CEO of Satancorp® and all its subsidiaries and satellite operations

SECTION I

GREED

While primarily concerned with the spheres of management, finance, and politics, the basic philosophy, and indeed everything else in this book holds true in all areas of life: it can be profitably applied to day-to-day dealings such as personal and household finances, family and friends, or even sports and hobbies, ensuring you achieve your full potential for dominance in everything you do.

The first stage in our program of self-development is the most important, as it concerns the core value from which all the Principles are derived—Greed.

Greed is the motivation behind any serious attempts at self-improvement, and recognition of this is the key to success. For too long, this vital incentive to accomplishment has had a bad press, and fulfillment has been denied to all but the brave few who bucked the trend (more often than not by seeking my help). But now the tide has turned, thanks to those pioneers of acquisitiveness, and avarice has become respectable; at least, in the circles I move in.

In the following section we will explore six positive lessons to be learned by cultivating a proactive appreciation of Greed, and the six guiding Principles by which you can benefit from it.

"Nothing succeeds
like excess"

Principle 1

GREED IS GOOD, GLUTTONY IS BETTER

Once we can overcome our prejudices against Greed and accept it as an indispensable motivating force, we can begin to adopt strategies to utilize it. I value it so highly that I've appointed my most trusted demon of greed, Mammon, to oversee its operations in my own organization.

Hunger—not just for food, but also for material wealth, luxury, and dominance in social hierarchies—is a natural instinct. It is the need to satisfy that hunger that drives us to achieve. A greater appetite will thus lead to greater achievement, and going beyond merely satisfying that hunger (i.e., being greedy) will lead to even greater success. Now, when did you last hear of someone overachieving? Right, never. There's no such thing as overachievement! But few people realize that it's likewise impossible to want too much. Therefore greed is good—and gluttony is even better. It stands to reason.

Of course, most of the time, there's only so much to go around, so somebody's got to lose out somewhere along the line. But it won't be the greediest. Oh no—he's more likely to be the top dog, and the thrifty guy with modest needs and expectations is going to be at the bottom of the heap. To paraphrase Karl Marx (who got it nearly right):

"From each according to his gullibility, to each according to his greed."

CASE STUDY: IVAN BOESKY AND MICHAEL MILKEN

Boesky, the "Great White Shark of Wall Street" is the guy who first came right out and said "Greed is good" at an address to the Berkeley Business School, and so became the inspiration for Gordon Gekko in the film "Wall Street," despite ending up in jail for insider trading six months after his famous speech.

Loser :-(

In a futile attempt at plea bargaining, he informed on his friend Milken, the "Junk-Bond King," who also ended up serving time for fraud and racketeering. Unlike Boesky (who disappeared from the scene—but I've still got his number), Milken didn't let that get in the way of his success: after serving a couple of years it was business as usual, and his net worth today is in excess of $2 billion.

That's my boy !!!

THE LESSON TO BE LEARNED

Keep that greed coming on, even if you have setbacks. Oh, and snitching per se is not a bad thing—only make sure you benefit from it.

PRINCIPLE I IN ACTION

As we consume, so Greed drives us to acquire. Thus, consumption leads to action; thrift leads to inaction. We can see (fig. i) that there comes a critical point when acquisition matches consumption: choices made here are crucial to success.

One option is to simply continue acquiring while maintaining consumption levels (fig. ii). In this scenario, acquisition will overtake consumption, building up reserves. And possession gives power: other poor saps will be approaching you for resources—at a price, of course, accelerating your acquisition curve.

Another, better, alternative is to keep increasing consumption (fig. iii)—it's not difficult once you get the hang of it—which will drive the need for further acquisition.

Avoid attempting to lower the consumption rate (fig. iv): before you know it you'll be caught in the downward spiral of the loser (see also page 149).

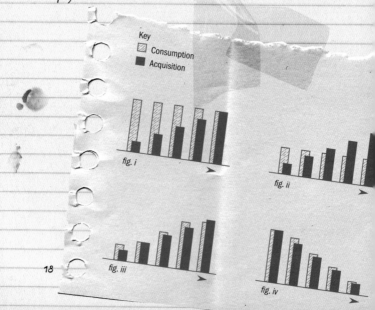

Key
Consumption
Acquisition

fig. i

fig. ii

fig. iii

fig. iv

18

Previous self-help manuals have made much of the paradigm I shall call the Preparation—Acquisition—Consumption cycle (PAC), which in my opinion will at best merely keep your head above water, struggling. This I replace with the Consumption—Acquisition—Satisfaction—Happiness cycle, which graphically illustrates the wisdom of the previous page's precepts.

THE CONSUMPTION—ACQUISITION—SATISFACTION—HAPPINESS CYCLE

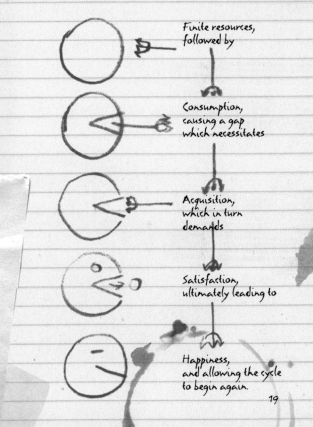

Finite resources, followed by

Consumption, causing a gap which necessitates

Acquisition, which in turn demands

Satisfaction, ultimately leading to

Happiness, and allowing the cycle to begin again.

19

WHY SETTLE FOR LESS?

A major reason why so many people fail to achieve their potential is that they actually believe some of the rubbish they're fed as if it were good advice. All sorts of maxims and homilies are repeated until they attain almost gospel status (as if that was a good thing!), but they only hamper real progress. One of the worst, in my humble opinion (humble? Me? What irony!), is "Be on your guard against all kinds of greed; for one's life does not consist in the abundance of possessions." What the hell kind of a message is that? Nobody got anywhere worth going by stopping at first base. So, forget all that down-home crap, and go for it. First and foremost, aim high. But also choose your targets carefully, and make sure you've got the right ammunition.

Vice is nice
LOL

CASE STUDY: DICK CHENEY

From lowly but promising beginnings as a drunk-driving draft-dodger, Cheney rose rapidly to become one of the most powerful and successful men on the planet. Keeping an eye on the main chance, he worked his way into the White House during the Ford administration, and just kept on making his way up, becoming Defense Secretary under George Bush Snr.

Undeterred by what could have been the lean years of the Clinton presidency, Dick moved into business, using knowledge and contacts from his previous job (including a little devil called Mammon) to get him appointed CEO of Halliburton in 1995. When he returned to politics as G.W. Bush's Vice President in 2000, he stepped down from the top job at Halliburton and took a back seat as the company's No. 2—just to show there would be no conflict of interest. Concentrating on his role as his country's second-in-command (hah! we all know who's really been running the show since then), he encouraged George W.'s invasion of Iraq,, which coincidentally landed Halliburton some nice juicy contracts. He learned it all from me ...

THE LESSON TO BE LEARNED

Aim for the most advantageous targets. Cheney has always aimed just high enough (apart from that unfortunate hunting accident): although he was nominally No. 2 in both Halliburton and the White House, he was always the one pulling the strings, and taking the benefits, but not ultimately responsible.

PRINCIPLE II IN ACTION

....

Taking a typical hierarchical corporate structure scenario (see diagram), we can easily see that there is a right and a wrong way to progress your career. On the left, there is the traditional merit-based promotion path: at every level you're forced to jump through hoops to reach the next rung of the ladder.

Note the possibility of ending up in a cycle of nonachievement at any level—or even dropping down the pecking order—if you're not up to cutting a few corners. Being competent at your job is not enough, and could condemn you to a lifetime of poorly paid misery and mediocrity. Remember, the road to Hell is paved with good intentions, and it's better to take the shortcut.

Running through the center of the organization, however, there is a middle way (shown here in red) which cuts through the obstacles and allows an accelerated rise without wasting time on tedious training or pointless experience in irrelevant departments. All it takes is naked ambition and chutzpah.

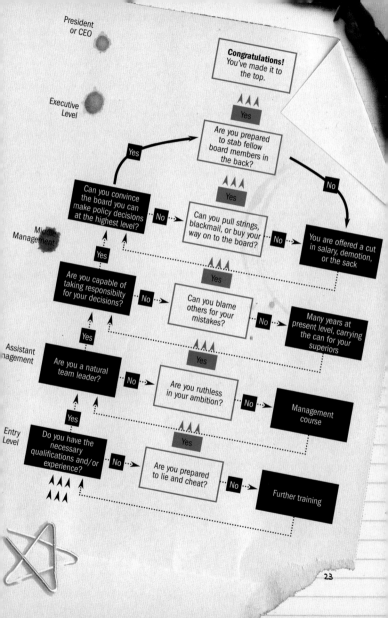

President
or CEO

Congratulations!
You've made it to
the top.

Executive
Level

▲▲▲ Yes

Are you prepared
to stab fellow
board members in
the back?

Yes

No

Can you convince
the board you can
make policy decisions
at the highest level?

No →

Can you pull strings,
blackmail, or buy your
way on to the board?

No →

You are offered a cut
in salary, demotion,
or the sack

Middle
Management

Yes

Are you capable of
taking responsibilty
for your decisions?

No →

▲▲▲ Yes

Can you blame
others for your
mistakes?

No →

Many years at
present level, carrying
the can for your
superiors

Yes

Assistant
Management

Are you a natural
team leader?

No →

▲▲▲ Yes

Are you ruthless
in your ambition?

No →

Management
course

Yes

Entry
Level

Do you have the
necessary
qualifications and/or
experience?

No →

▲▲▲ Yes

Are you prepared
to lie and cheat?

No →

Further training

▲▲▲
▲▲▲

Principle iii

IT AIN'T FAIR

Let's get one thing straight: life isn't fair. Period. The trick is to make it unfair to your advantage rather than someone else's. In almost every situation, whether it's negotiating a business deal, settling a dispute with a friend or colleague, or even dividing up the household chores, someone's going to end up worse off. To make sure that it isn't you, get your retaliation in first: start your negotiations from a position of strength by claiming what you want at the outset, so the other guy's having to play catch-up and pleading with you for concessions. You might not get everything you want, but hey, I did say life ain't fair.

THE FAIR-SHARE MYTH

"Fair" shares:
everyone gets only one
bite of the cherry

There are still those who would have you
believe that there's plenty to go round, so long
as we all only take our fair share. This is
dangerously misleading. If you don't grab
what you can, someone else will. And some
deluded souls are happy to let you do it, content
with their meager share. Think of it as a public
service to them. After all, somebody's got to take up all the excess.
Now, you might be tempted to wait until everyone's taken what they want,
then scoop up the remainder—but why tempt fate? If you can get in there
first and take the pick of the crop (and some), you don't run the risk of
picking up the leftovers.

PRINCIPLE III IN ACTION

Time for a little parable to illustrate the point. At a meeting recently, I was offered cookies with my coffee; there were two on the plate, one plain and not very appetizing, the other much bigger and with chocolate chips. As the guest, I was given first choice, so naturally took the better one—and my host was obviously pissed by this. I asked him what he would have done if he'd had first pick, and he assured me he would, out of politeness, have taken the plain cookie. "No problem then," I replied, "you got it."

When it comes to negotiating, make sure any unfairness is skewed in your favor—and if it looks like the deal is going to be equitable, rethink the framework of the transaction. There's always some way to get a bigger piece of the cake. Slice it any way you like, you can always get the top layer. The frosting's always the best part.

Resource distribution is seldom symmetrical: take advantage of this anomaly

Be inventive when it comes to agreeing parameters

Principle iv

THERE ARE PERKS IN BUSINESS CLASS, AND EVEN MORE IN FIRST CLASS

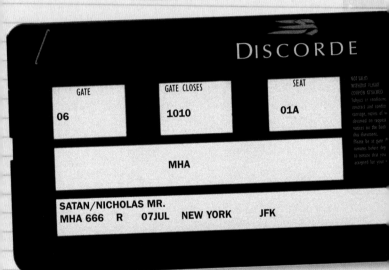

It should go without saying at this stage in the course that Greed will help you to always get that little bit extra.

But there's no need to hunt around for freebies, or haggle to get a better deal. That sounds like purgatory to me (and you'll have plenty of that in due course). Take a tip from the frequent traveler: push for an upgrade, and you'll get all the extras offered to you. On a plate. And with champagne.

The higher up the scale you go, the better the perks—and those fringe benefits can really add up once you adopt a high-flying lifestyle.

But most importantly, if you travel first class through life, you are treated with respect. You'll get priority treatment when booking hotels, flights, tickets for the game, and just about everything else. Don't worry about payment, either. If you've established yourself as a first-class customer, it is all put on your account and can be dealt with later. Much later. Maybe.

Take a simple example. You're on a business trip out of town and need somewhere to spend the night. Option one is a cheap hotel on Skid Row: lousy choice, as you'll have to produce cash up front, and then spend a sleepless night worrying about how much you've been ripped off for this uncomfortable, bug-ridden hellhole without even an ensuite. Option two is the mid-range motel: better, but still no cigar—although it's clean and comfortable, it's making a dent in your credit card and you've still got to pay extra for the minibar, room service, and phone calls. Option three is the five star: now we're talking. A luxurious suite with complimentary drinks and food, unlimited use of the gym, sauna, and massage parlor, and staff at your beck and call. And the bill's sent to your company. No contest.

MILE HIGH AIRWAYS

NAME OF PASSENGER
SATAN/NICHOLAS MR.
MHA 666

FROM
LONDON   **LHR**
NEW YORK   **JFK**

CARRIER / FLIGHT
MHA 666   CLASS / DATE **R**   **07JUL**   TIME **1030**

GATE
6   **1010**   SEAT **EXC**
          01A

PASSENGER TICKET AND BAGGAGE CHECK

PRINCIPLE IV IN ACTION

The old cliché "If you pay peanuts, you get monkeys" is often thrown around by fat cats who feel they need to justify their inflated salaries, but there's a grain of truth in it. I prefer to think of it as "If you accept peanuts, you get treated like a monkey." Unless, of course, the peanuts are served with your complimentary cocktails in the first-class lounge.

A comparative analysis of three contrasting business-capitalization strategies:

Mr. A, whose one-man business has hit hard times, is in desperate need of an injection of cash, is in desperate goes to his bank for a loan. He refused immediately. In desperation, he turns to a loan shark, commits himself to a crippling rate of interest and within months finds himself even deeper in debt, with the added worry of the local mob demanding ever-increasing payments.

VERDICT: FAILURE

Mr. B, who runs a small but successful manufacturing business, tries to get finance for modest expansion, and visits his local bank. He is anxious to show how careful he is with his finances, and tries to demonstrate how he is keeping costs to a minimum, but only manages to secure a small loan with the assets of his firm as security, and the prospect of financial ruin if he defaults on the deal.

VERDICT: PARTIAL SUCCESS

Mr. C, however, has bigger ideas. Although his business does not yet actually produce anything, he approaches the bank with an outrageously expensive scheme, the only assets being promises from other lenders. He meets the bankers at a prestigious hotel, arrives in a chauffeur-driven limousine, wearing an outrageously expensive suit and conspicuously extravagant jewelry, and is loan of more than he could possibly Not only does he get an unsecured need, but he gets VIP treatment: free lunches at which to discuss the deal, introductions to yet more potential investors, and an invitation to join the local country club.

VERDICT: OUTRIGHT SUCCESS

Principle v

THE MORALS OF MORE

Once you show a talent for acquisition, people will be falling over themselves to offer you more.

Got an obscenely large bank balance?
Here's a loan.

Got a rapacious and money-hungry business?
Let me invest my life savings.

And it's not just money—conspicuous success in any field attracts more of the same. Got a lively social scene with celebs, and movers and shakers? You must come round to dinner.

Made your name through appearances on reality TV?
Here's a book deal and your own talk show.

Take a look at the top-performing companies in the world's stock exchanges. Nine times out of ten, their share prices have precious little to do with how the firm's doing: investors buy into what they perceive as a successful business, based on... guess what? What everybody's investing in. Inevitably, this helps enhance the company's reputation, and so attracts more investment. Hell, you don't even have to produce anything. Except wealth, of course.

CASE STUDY: THE DOT COM BOOM 1996–2000

The arrival of the internet sparked off a rash of highly successful new ventures in the 1990s, attracting investment on a scale not seen since the heady days of Wall Street in the late 1920s. Analysts proclaimed these dot com businesses introduced a "new paradigm" in investment strategy (for which read: "a new way to raise money from reckless hyping of low-value, high-risk companies"), and venture capitalists enthusiastically leapt into a bull market (and I mean bull) where share prices reached record levels—largely for companies with no record of success, or even yet to make any profit at all. All sorts of half-baked ideas were floated (reminiscent of schemes like the Union Pacific Railroad in 1872), and despite the risk traded at ludicrously inflated and ever-increasing prices, creating a new breed of dot com millionaires. Marvelous! Simply boost a stock with enough hype and investors will rush at it like lemmings. Who do you think was behind all this? And the Wall Street scandal, and Lehman Brothers ...

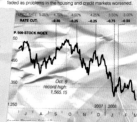

Lower Rates: Not Yet the Tonic

The Federal Reserve has lowered its benchmark interest rate five times since September. Stocks have tended to surge in anticipation of those cuts, even hitting a record in October. But the rallies have faded as problems in the housing and credit markets worsened.

THE LESSON TO BE LEARNED

No one ever lost money by underestimating the intelligence of investors.

PRINCIPLE V IN ACTION

The correlation between the reputation of a business and investment in it (regardless of its actual value) can be seen in *fig. i*, which shows the exponential rise in the perceived value, and thus the price of shares.

In *fig. ii*, the combination of mounting confidence and a steadily rising share price leads to a similar accelerating curve in the potential wealth of the entrepreneur, which bears no relation to the productivity of his company.

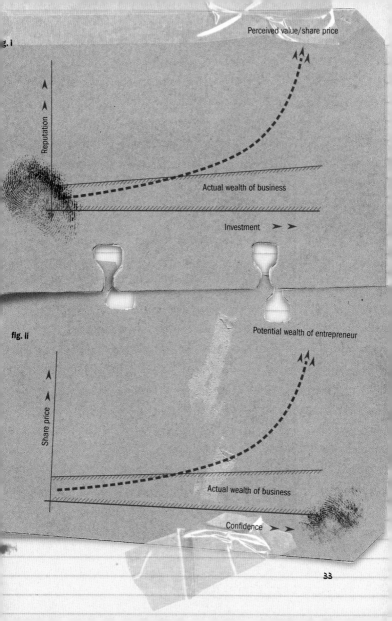

fig. i

Perceived value/share price

Reputation

Actual wealth of business

Investment

Potential wealth of entrepreneur

fig. ii

Share price

Actual wealth of business

Confidence

33

Principle vi

THE FROSTING ON THE CAKE

Some of the worst of the self-help manuals—you know, the ones that give pious advice about leading a good life and virtue being its own reward, that kind of bullshit—put a deal of emphasis on job satisfaction, and I have to admit, they've got a point. But not the way they have it. I don't mean basking smugly in the glow of a job well done. No, Greed brings its own rewards too, but in ways that are sometimes overlooked.

The successfully Greedy person is, of course, materially better off and can enjoy a more comfortable lifestyle but, more than that, he or she can get an inordinate amount of pleasure from simply knowing they're better off. Especially if they got there at someone else's expense. Don't underestimate the joy of Schadenfreude, the delight in seeing others not getting what you've got is "wunderbar"!

It's a win–win situation—the better you're doing, the better you feel about it; and when you feel good, you do better. More than that, the satisfaction you're getting from wealth and success does wonders for your confidence and self-esteem, which in turn not only promotes even greater success, but also makes you a more attractive person. You'll be in demand in a way that no loser could even dream about, and in no time will have a host of fiendish acolytes.

This domino effect snowballs, and before you know it will have mushroomed into a situation where you can't go wrong.

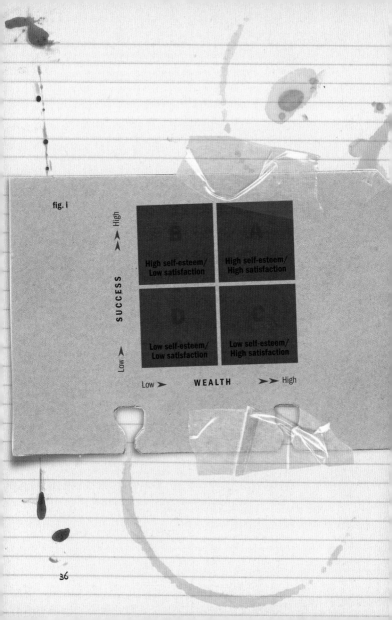

fig. i

SUCCESS

High

Low

B
High self-esteem/
Low satisfaction

A
High self-esteem/
High satisfaction

D
Low self-esteem/
Low satisfaction

C
Low self-esteem/
High satisfaction

Low   WEALTH   High

PRINCIPLE VI IN ACTION

The Wealth/Success coordinates in *fig. i* generate a straightforward model of four distinct outcome scenarios. Each of these has its own resultant satisfaction/self-esteem pattern, with D (Low satisfaction and self-esteem) being the least desirable, rising through moderately acceptable situations at C and B, to the ideal paradigm, A, where satisfaction and self-esteem are at their ultimate.

In *fig. ii*, achieving a peak of wealth (1) leads inevitably to a pinnacle of satisfaction (2) and promotes heightened success (3), skipping the troughs that low-achievers need to cross. The process then becomes cyclical, with soaring success producing yet more wealth. It must be remembered, however, that this is made possible only on a foundation of acquisition (4) which is dependent on greed (5).

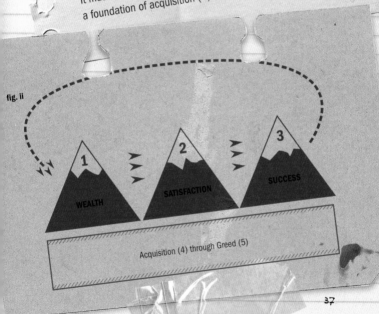

fig. ii

THE SIX PRINCIPLES OF GREED IN A NUTSHELL

i   You can never have too much of a good thing

ii   There is always room at the top

iii   All is fair in love and business

iv   There is such a thing as a free lunch

v   To him that hath more shall be given

vi   Money doesn't buy happiness—
it just comes with the package

TRIDENT TESTED

SECTION II

LUST

Having established that Greed is the core motivation, we must now move on to identify how this can best be exploited: simply recognizing a capacity for consumption is not enough. Nobody gets to the top of the heap by just taking what's on offer; you've always got to want more.

In order to progress, it is important to assess the level of your desire, and where necessary increase it to match your outcome expectations. The key tool at this stage is Lust, in all its many glorious forms. We're talking Basic Instincts here—appetites, libido, and above all the Lust for Power.

Powerful People are always passionate about Power—from this observation we can clearly see that Power is in direct proportion to Passion, and by extrapolation that the Lust which fuels that Passion has a crucial bearing on Achievement. The more passionate and conspicuous your desires, the more they will be recognized and satisfied. It's not the saint who gets the girls, it's the horny little devil. Take it from me.

In this section we will examine the six steps to developing a healthy Lust Life, at each stage relating this to a practical, goal-centered application of the Principles.

"Whatever you want, you've got to want it bad"

Principle 1

TRUST LUST

Some damn fools tell you that the road to success is all about hard work and doing stuff you don't want to. What garbage. If you want to get up there with the Powerful People, start by thinking what you want out of life. Yeah, right—the really important things, like money, influence, and a vigorous love life. These are basic instincts, and once you can recognize that they're what are really calling the shots, and learn to trust your appetites, you can begin to channel that instinctive drive into achieving your goals and attracting like-minded fiends to enjoy them with. It's Lust, not virtue, that is its own reward.

CASE STUDY: HUGH HEFNER

Founder of Playboy Enterprises, Hugh Hefner built his empire by going for what he wanted most—fame, fortune, and sex—and succeeded admirably (with a little help from yours truly, of course). Satisfying all his lusts, he published a magazine featuring nude pics of Marilyn Monroe in 1953, the first issue of "Playboy," and thus began a career of making money out of what he likes doing best. And not only money: the Playboy club brought him popularity, too, and anyone who is anyone hankers after an invite to the frequent parties at his home, Playboy Mansion—a surefire way of winning fiends. As for the sex and power, well, over the years he's had his pick of the Playmates and continues to enjoy them even in his eighties. By trusting his lustful instincts, Hefner has made sure he's one happy bunny.

THE LESSON TO BE LEARNED

Let your lust lead the way.

PRINCIPLE I IN ACTION

There are a number of variables that must be taken into account when assessing the importance of Lust to a successful and fulfilling life. On the one hand, there are the messages you're sending out about your desire to achieve, which are (as we shall see in greater detail on pages 58-61) proportional to the degree of influence you can wield; on the other hand, there is what you can hope to profitably achieve.

In other words, quality of life is dependent on a combination of sex appeal and power, moderated only by the amount of yield. This can be enhanced by filtering out negative factors in a process of positive expectation, optimism, and attraction.

Put simply, what you get out of an opening depends not just on what you put in—but how you put it in and what you do with it.

QUALITY OF LIFE QUOTIENT

$$QQ = \frac{(S+1) \times (P+1)}{(Y)^2}$$

seen against a favorable background:

OPTIMISM	ATTRACTION	EXPECTATION

provides an attractive prospect:

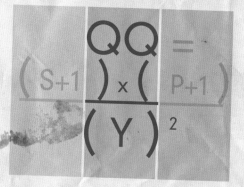

Where:

QQ	= Quality of Life quotient
S	= Sex appeal
P	= Power
Y	= Yield

Principle ii

THE SIX CAUSES OF LUST

Understanding the various forms of Lust and their origins helps to develop a focused strategy for reaching your goals. The six principal Lust incentives—Wealth and Property, Power and Sex, Fame and Popularity—are all equally important, and interconnected. Each provides a motivation in its own right, but more than that, each fosters the strength and potency of the others.

The golden rule is to position yourself at the convergent point of these six causal attractions to maximize your personal expansion. In other words, just be totally self-centered. It's always worked for me.

Remember—

"*I*" is the center of "*DESIRES.*"

CASE STUDY: GIOVANNI GIACOMO CASANOVA

Once he'd got himself expelled from a seminary (just after I first met him—maybe that had something to do with it!), Casanova embarked on the career that he was most suited to. At various times a musician, professional gambler, and investor (usually using other people's money), the director of the Paris lottery, soldier, spy, diplomat, and writer, he is better known today for his sexual conquests and scurrilous autobiography. He was the darling of 18th-century European society, counting among his friends aristocrats, royalty, and intellectuals (and, you'll have guessed, my good self). If he'd followed his original choice of career in the church, he would have been just another miserable nobody—and I told him so. Happily, he let Lust get the better of him, and his name is now immortalized as a synonym for "libertine."

THE LESSON TO BE LEARNED

Don't focus your Lusts too narrowly.

The more, the merrier.

PRINCIPLE II IN ACTION

The expansionary power of the six causes of Lust can be clearly seen in this diagram, with the complementary forces of Wealth and Property, Power and Sex, and Fame and Popularity working in harmony on the appropriately placed central Self.

Causes of Lust

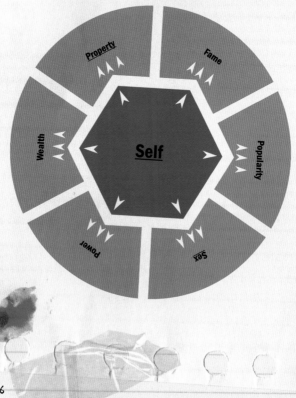

Here, we can see the interaction of the incentivizing Lusts, forming a strong cyclical pattern, reinforced by a framework of subsidiary connectivity and cause/effect situations.

**The cycle of stimuli
and resultant motivations**

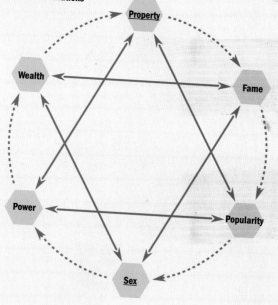

Principle iii

CRYING OUT FOR IT

Now here's something they don't teach at business school: some people are just asking to be screwed. You know the type—inadequate, ineffective, and struggling to make ends meet—and pitifully grateful for any attention you give them. But just because they're an easy target doesn't mean you shouldn't make the most of the situation. In fact, they're so obviously screwable, I've got a sneaking feeling they actually welcome it.

So go ahead, enjoy. Think of it as mutually beneficial; they get the screwing they deserve, and you get their assets and probably another loyal fiend. Plus the pleasure of seeing them suffer.

CASE STUDY: MARQUIS DE SADE

Donatien Alphonse François de Sade needs little introduction: he was a pornographer, hedonist, cruel debaucher, pedophile, and convicted felon who ended his days in an asylum—an all-round good guy. He also managed to be both a revolutionary and an aristocrat (a great trick if you can pull it off), which so impressed me that I got my boys to introduce an "administrative error" to save him from the guillotine. One of my favorite clients, in fact, with no virtues to stain his character, and a popular figure down here since his demise. He shamelessly abused his powerful position and exploited other people's weaknesses, but, best of all, he really enjoyed watching them squirm. I can't understand how "sadism" got to be a dirty word.

THE LESSON TO BE LEARNED

Squeeze them till the pips squeak.

Of course, you have to offer some kind of incentive to exploit vulnerability. This needn't be too much of a drain on your resources, however: everybody has a price, and you'd be surprised how cheap most people come.

The first step is to select your targets and identify their weaknesses. Dangle the right bait in front of them and they'll go for it hook, line, and sinker. Once you've got them hooked, you can reel them in, kicking and screaming (but not for long—they soon calm down and accept the inevitable), and you've got it on a plate. I do it all the time, and the poor souls have always thanked me for it.

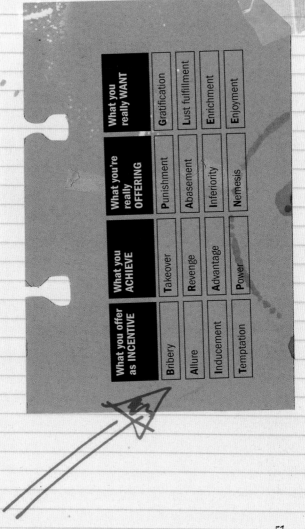

What you offer as INCENTIVE	What you ACHIEVE	What you're really OFFERING	What you really WANT
Bribery	Takeover	Punishment	Gratification
Allure	Revenge	Abasement	Lust fulfillment
Inducement	Advantage	Inferiority	Enrichment
Temptation	Power	Nemesis	Enjoyment

51

MEN ARE FROM BARS, WOMEN ENVY* PENIS

....

The fundamental differences between the two sexes' *modi operandi* are frequently overlooked in self-help manuals. The archetypal testosterone-fueled male is something of a cliché, as is the compliant female, but not without foundation.

A quick look at a list of Powerful People reveals a preponderance of men, and the image they convey is that of the hard-nosed, thrusting go-getter who likes to be on top. Men-only institutions reinforce this advantage, providing stiff opposition and the erection of barriers to female participation.

The few women who reach their peak, it has to be said, have generally refused to take this lying down and have adopted many elements of this macho persona. Some, however, have tried thinking outside the box and (as we shall see in the following pages) discovered that power can also be wielded in more subtle ways.

Lessons can be learned by studying both approaches, and playing to your strengths.

*This is a specific form of envy dealt with here only for its relevance to Lust. For a fuller discussion of Envy, see Section V (pages 109–132)

PRINCIPLE IV IN ACTION

....

The differences in approach and outcome between the sexes become obvious when seen graphically.

In the upper graph, the male satisfaction-seeking drive (a) shows a high level of interest with only moderate fluctuation, while the progress of its fulfillment (b) has a markedly more rise/fall dynamic; note that the rise at (x) is fundamentally unsustainable, and if allowed to pass its critical point (y) before satisfactorily entering into any venture will simply come to nothing.

In distinct contrast, the lower graph shows the characteristic curves associated with female targeting/yield parameters: in both the pursuit of objectives (c) and rate of gratification (d) there is an initial sharp increase followed by a rapid loss of impetus once a peak has been achieved, followed by a gentler rhythm of activity.

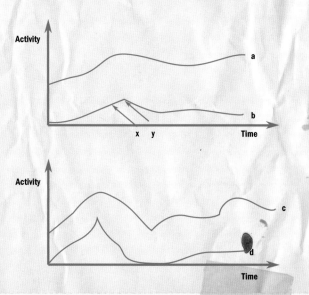

CLIMBING THE GREASY POLE—SEDUCTION & INGRATIATION

You probably never thought you'd hear me say this, but it really is helpful to get in touch with your feminine side. I don't mean that sloppy caring, sharing, Mother Earth baloney—no way. What I'm advocating is the seductive temptress thing which casts a spell that can be exploited. You know, the step-into-my-parlor spider-and-fly situation.

Using feminine wiles to appear alluring is yet another way of arousing Lust in others which you can then turn to your advantage; you can make some advantageous liaisons on your way to the top, and gain power over those who are not up to it. That goes for ambitious females as well as males—all too often women overlook their inherent talents, and men don't learn from situations when they've been had. Sometimes, flattery will get you everywhere.

CASE STUDY: LUCREZIA BORGIA

A real sweetheart, Lucrezia. No, I mean it—she had a natural flair for utilizing her assets, and needed only a little encouragement from me, which I was happy to offer such an enchanting lady. Of course she had a good start in life, being daughter of a Pope (that doesn't happen every day) and brought up in a ruthlessly ambitious family, but, being a mere woman, she could have ended up on the sidelines if she hadn't turned on the charm. That got her three influential marriages (and a hell of a lot of useful affairs) and a reputation as a femme fatale which she enhanced with a poisoning or two.

THE LESSON TO BE LEARNED

Where there's a wile, there's a way.

Often, what you want is out there waiting, and rather than pursuing it you should make it come to you. The trick is to provide the right attraction, just to sugar the pill, in order to draw the objective into your sphere of influence. The closer it gets, the more alluring you should be, until it reaches the point of no return. A useful rule of thumb is to employ my six-step plan of allure, so that your victim is:

1 Aware

2 Intrigued

3 Interested

4 Fascinated

5 Tempted

6 Hooked

WEALTH

POPULARITY

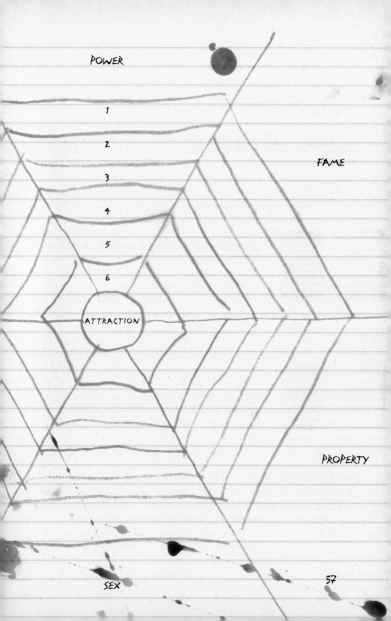

POWER is sexy, SEX is power

To round off this section on correctly identifying, cultivating, and utilizing your Lust, we come to perhaps the most important of its Principles, one that will enable the user to convert Desire into Control.

Henry Kissinger (and he should know, I taught him well) once said "Power is the greatest aphrodisiac;" what he didn't let on is that the converse is also true. Powerful People have voracious appetites which they satisfy at every opportunity—not just because they can, but because they must. And libidinous people become dominant players when they indulge their cravings often—doing so becomes a series of conquests.

Successful people are attractive, and attractive people have the capacity to become successful. But more than that, Powerful People are insatiable, and insatiable people invariably achieve Power. This is probably the most important of the Lust Principles, and should be thoroughly understood before you attempt to put it into practice.

Think of it this way: in a pack of dogs, the leader gets to mate with all the females—the other males don't get a shot—and, guess what, he got the job by showing that he wanted to mate with all the females. In a nutshell, if you want to screw your way to the top, you've got to really want to screw your way to the top, and let everybody know you're up for it.

Put in scientific terms,
the principle is simple:

Power is proportional to Libido

More specifically:

$$P = L^2 \times W$$

(where P is Power, L is Libido, and W is the Will to use it)

from which it follows that:

$$L = \sqrt{P/W}$$

PRINCIPLE VI IN ACTION

In order to exploit the full potential of your Lust, it's vitally important to rise to the challenge. You not only have to crave success, but also anticipate a successful outcome. The negative attitudes of low expectations and lack of desire mean you'll end up pissing away your chances.

On the other hand, once you see an opening that appeals, by allowing the power and passion of your Lust to swell your confidence, you'll be conspicuously more penetrative, and so will impress those around you as up-and-coming.

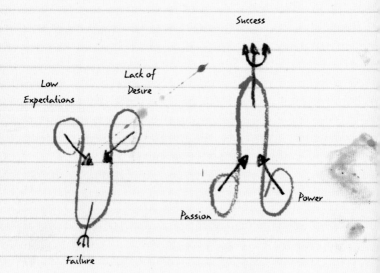

In exercising the energy of Lust, it is important to avoid overexertion. The rule here is: minimum input, maximum output. To ensure your libidinous efforts are not wasted, a simple shift of the power base gives a mechanical advantage—putting out over a wider base brings increased rewards and satisfaction.

The Balance of Power

Enticement
and
self-promotion

Influence
and
attraction

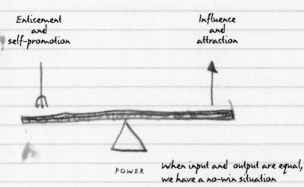

POWER

When input and output are equal, we have a no-win situation

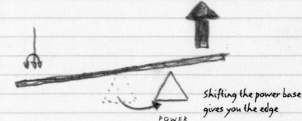

Shifting the power base gives you the edge

POWER

The six Principles of LUST in a nutshell

i   Where there's a wile there's a way

ii   Lust is a many-splendored thing

iii   No pain, no gain—
their pain, your gain

iv   Take it like a man

v   Familiarity breeds attempt

vi   Help yourself

666

SLOTH

Where in the previous two sections we have been considering the incentives (Greed) and motivations (Lust) that lead us on the path to self-improvement, we must now move on to examining the strategies for achieving our goals.

Central to this is the whole business of managing time and resources—and that's where Sloth comes into its own. Unfortunately, Sloth is often misunderstood, and thought to be an obstacle to achievement. What's more, a lot of self-help gurus extol the virtues (virtues? Pah!) of hard work. In fact, quite the opposite is true, as we shall see.

So, forget all that Protestant work ethic bullshit. That was only ever meant to keep the workers at it so the bosses could sit back and watch the money roll in. I should know, as I developed the idea in the first place. One law for the rich, another for the poor, as I keep telling my clients.

It's just common sense really, like all the best ideas. A real appreciation of the value of Sloth helps you to avoid any unnecessary effort, and allows you to achieve optimum work–leisure and responsibility–reward ratios.

"It works, you don't"

Principle 1

IF IT'S HARD WORK, YOU'RE DOING IT WRONG

The first thing to recognize is that effort is inversely proportional to reward. That is, the harder you work, the less you get out of it—and the less you work, the more you'll gain. No, really.

Think about it—Joe Six-Pack works maybe 40 hours a week, sends his wife and kids out to work, does all his own home repairs, and still has to moonlight with a second job to make ends meet; his boss spends a couple of hours a day in the office and the rest on the golf course or dining at his club, and has enough dough (and more) to pay for staff in his houses and apartments, and to keep his wife in diamonds and his children in fancy schools. Which one is your role model?

	Joe Six-Pack	Fat Cat
Hours/Week	60 (plus occasional overtime)	20 (max)
Annual Salary	$20,000	$5 million (plus bonuses, share options, perks, etc.)
Evening	Moonlighting as cab driver, security guard, etc.	Dinner parties, country club, night clubs
Weekends	Fixing up the house, maybe a couple of beers in front of a game on TV	Entertaining guests on the yacht, or at the second home
Vacation	Two weeks with the in-laws	Regular month-long breaks at swanky resorts worldwide

CASE STUDY: GEORGE W. BUSH

It's tough at the top. Being leader of the free world can sure take it out of you. But rest assured, the Presidents of the USA have established a work—life balance that guarantees they're in good shape. Ronald Reagan set the standard by taking a record 436 days vacation during his two terms as president (that's 54 and a half days per year), an example emulated, and bettered, by George Bush Snr's 543 days off in a single term. George W. followed in his daddy's footsteps, spending more than a quarter of his time at Camp David, Kennebunkport, or the ranch in Crawford, Texas. Compare his highly paid three months and more with the average American's 13 days paid vacation time, and then decide for yourself who's the village idiot.

Vacation maestro!

PRINCIPLE I IN ACTION

In strategic planning of any venture, whether it be business, finance, or social, the golden rule is to follow the path of least effort, greatest reward.

Since reward and effort are inversely proportional, in any given venture

$$R = V / E$$

(where R is reward, V is the venture, and E is effort)

and we can immediately see a law of diminishing returns: the greater the effort made, the smaller the resultant reward; and conversely, the smaller the reward, the greater the effort needed to achieve it. But (and here's the crux of the theory), conversely

$$E = V / R$$

so the effort diminishes as the reward increases.

In practical terms, this means that you're going to be slaving away if you aim for too little, but if you go for bust you'll have an easy ride—and if you work your butt out you'll have little to show for it, but if you sit back and let somebody else do the grunt work you'll reap the rewards.

It may seem that my diabolic methods merely confront us with the horns of a dilemma, but remember that the Devil looks after his own! The elements in the matrix below provide an at-a-glance reference to the strategies and tactics (dealt with in more detail in the following pages) that will extricate you from any situation vis à vis rocks and hard places. Between you and me, there's always an easy way out.

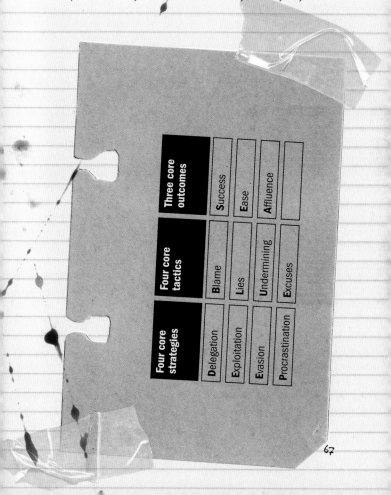

Four core strategies	Four core tactics	Three core outcomes
Delegation	Blame	Success
Exploitation	Lies	Ease
Evasion	Undermining	Affluence
Procrastination	Excuses	

Principle ii

ONE-MINUTE MANAGEMENT—
DELEGATE, DELEGATE,
DELEGATE

Unless you're the lowest of the low (and let's face it, you wouldn't be reading this if you were—hell, you wouldn't even be able to afford it) there's always somebody lower down the pecking order. That means there's always somebody you can dump the worst of your workload on. It's not just that they're in no position to refuse, but if you pitch it right, they'll be only too happy to help out and take on some extra responsibility.

This works with your peers too: a carefully worded request works wonders in clearing items from your to-do list, at the same time gaining you reputation as a team player.* And, once you've mastered the technique, the Principle can even be applied to superiors (if you've still got any—the ideal is, of course, to be at the top of any hierarchy).

* Much admired in some circles, but a greatly overrated, and even dangerous quality, if you ask me. Goes against every Principle in the book. My book, anyway. Don't be tempted.

PRINCIPLE II IN ACTION

It's not just in business that you'll find this strategy useful.
The Principle holds true wherever you face tasks that get in the
way of your leisure time—from the office to your social club and
even at home—only the method has to be modified slightly to
suit the situation.

SIX WAYS TO SLOTH

IF YOU'RE A:		THEN:
Manager		Delegate
Colleague		Offload
Member of social group		Nominate
Friend		Persuade
Spouse		Flatter
Parent		Bribe

Principle iii

EXPLOITS IN EXPLOITATION

Now we've seen the importance of delegation, it's time to look at how this works in greater detail. It's not just a question of having plenty of underlings—although I didn't get where I am today without making certain there were plenty of lesser demons and fiends to do my bidding—but also finding their weak spot. In general, this comes down to either their greed, or their stupidity.

Exploiting greed is easy; you just offer them the promise of a good return for their efforts. But oddly, when you're exploiting stupidity, you have to be a bit more clever. If you've got a job that needs doing, get staff to do it for you. If you pay them less than you're getting for it, you've made a profit by doing nothing. You might be tempted to pay them more as an incentive to work harder, but don't—pay them less! They'll need to work longer hours to earn the same: ergo you get more out of them. The threat of losing their jobs helps stop them from slacking.

In middle management and above, this means appointing people below you to do the stuff you should be doing. The higher up you get, the less you do, and the more people you have to offload on to. The ultimate, of course, is to be at the top of the tree, where everybody is working for you—you don't do a thing.

Best of all, the more people you've got slaving for you, the higher your perceived status.

CASE STUDY: CHARLES PONZI

Ponzi (aka Carl or Carlo Ponei or Bianchi), the unsung hero of get-rich-quick schemes, arrived in the US from Italy in 1903 with $2.50, and was jailed soon after for a fraudulent banking scam and importing illegal immigrants. He saw the error of his ways during his time inside (which was when he first approached me for guidance), and on his release, went straight. Straight to the Post Office, where he cashed some international postal reply coupons from Italy, making a profit of around 400%—then sent agents to Italy to buy more and encouraged investors to join in the scheme, with promises of a 50% return. People flocked to buy into this arbitrage scam, and Ponzi made a killing. He was a multimillionaire by 1920, letting his agents handle the huge numbers of investors, who in fact were being paid by... yet more investors—Ponzi had long ago given up buying and selling postal reply coupons. And so it would have continued, but for the probing of a nosy journalist who brought the whole deck of cards down (and of course he wasn't tipped off by me).

THE LESSON TO BE LEARNED

If you've got a good idea, find someone else to do the grunt work—on commission, not salary, naturally—and find enough suckers to finance it.

PRINCIPLE III IN ACTION

In a typical business situation, a manager (A) will delegate a task to more than one subordinate (B). Because they consider they have a sufficient workload, they in turn will delegate tasks to the next level down (C), and so on, until the lowest level is reached. The task is thus distributed among the workforce, leaving the manager (A) to enjoy the time he's freed for himself, and the power he now has over his inferiors.

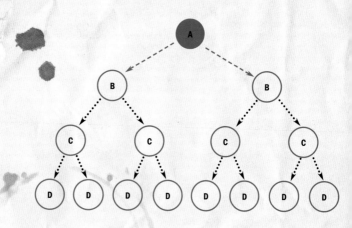

The elegance of this model of exploitation can be seen at its best in its most successful form, Multi-Level Marketing, where franchises are sold to budding entrepreneurs who are then responsible for day-to-day operations. A team of regional managers oversees operations, reporting back to the board who merely rubber-stamp the business and bank the profits, leaving virtually nothing for the top man to do—except get richer.

Chain of command and flow of resources in polyhedronic hierarchies

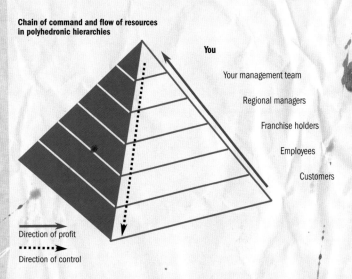

You

Your management team

Regional managers

Franchise holders

Employees

Customers

→ Direction of profit

••••••••→ Direction of control

THE BUCK STOPS WHERE?

Just as you can offload your workload (see pages 70–3), you can also shift the responsibility. Then, if things go belly up, you've got someone to blame, and it's their job on the line, not yours. Of course, if it all comes up smelling of roses, you should take all the credit—you were the supervising genius after all.

This may need a small amount of foresight and planning, but it's well worth it in terms of avoiding the extra work that failure can bring. Abdicating responsibility and shifting the blame not only avoids embarrassment and loss of respect, but it also means you don't have to clear up the mess. Anyway, it's easy enough to find a potential fall guy; there's always some ambitious loser who'll jump at the chance to take on the extra responsibility. That's how I got to be surrounded by sycophantic demons—where did you think the terms "whipping-boy" and "scapegoat" came from?

THE LESSON TO BE LEARNED

If your ambition takes you to the top, make sure you cover your ass by allocating all your responsibilities to your subordinates.

To Nik,
with best wishes
JOE

CASE STUDY: POLITICAL HIERARCHIES

Under a dictator, it's easy to see a "top-down" hierarchy where the president/monarch/emperor appoints ministers to take the rap when his or her policies fail (an execution or two doesn't go amiss either). But it's also true in so-called democracies: even though representatives are elected, the most ambitious among them will elbow their way to positions of power, and then allot responsibilities to those under them (this is a strategy I've advocated to clients of mine from Caligula through Stalin to Margaret Thatcher). A really great leader can take all the credit for policies that actually work, and have a ready-made whipping-boy for the ones that go horribly wrong.

PRINCIPLE IV IN ACTION

When faced with the possibility of being blamed for any action, it is useful to have a number of credible responses to criticism (from the "blamer") to deflect the responsibility, and also some tactics for ensuring that the eventual recipient of the blame (the "blamee") can't implicate you in any way.

A selection of possible blamer-directed responsibility-evasion techniques, and some blamee-oriented accountability-delegation processes can be seen in the chart opposite, but you should evolve your own personalized recrimination-aversion strategy which, in time, will become second nature.

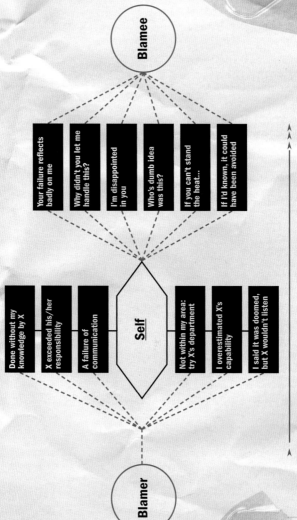

Blamee

Your failure reflects badly on me

Why didn't you let me handle this?

I'm disappointed in you

Who's dumb idea was this?

If you can't stand the heat...

If I'd known, it could have been avoided

Done without my knowledge by X

X exceeded his/her responsibility

A failure of communication

Self

Not within my area: try X's department

I overestimated X's capability

I said it was doomed, but X wouldn't listen

Direction of responsibility

Blamer

Principle v

NEVER STAND IF YOU CAN SIT, NEVER SIT IF YOU CAN LIE

Is your road to success paved with good intentions? Then it's time to put a stop to that, or there's no telling where it will lead you. Drop the good-guy image and admit to yourself that you really don't want to do all that stuff. Whatever you're doing, there's always an easier way of doing it—and that includes just not doing it at all.

So, get down to prioritizing your to-do list, sifting out all the chores you can offload, and then see if there's any way of not doing the rest. If it's a question of division of labor, make sure you're the one doing the dividing, and allocate yourself zilch. But if you're really put on the spot, consult your Blackberry; you can always plead the excuse of having a subsequent engagement.

Another useful tactic, but one that needs a little preparation, is to arrange your vacations, lunch breaks, dental appointments, visits to the executive washroom, etc. to coincide with periods of maximum activity.

FAVORITE DISPLACEMENT ACTIVITIES:

1. Making coffee
2. Pretending to read
3. Playing solitaire on the computer
4. Arranging my desk (especially adding to the elastic band ball)
5. Walking around the office making sure everyone else is working
6. Checking emails for links to the latest online jokes and videos
7. Doodling in the margins of important documents
8. Lunch
9. Playing with the printer/photocopier/shredder
10. Drawing up lists of my favorite things

But the simplest answer is to ignore it all—if you postpone any action long enough, there's a good chance someone else will notice and do it themselves, or even better, that nobody will notice it didn't get done. The noble art of procrastination is much maligned, and far from being the thief of time (what idiot thought up that dumb homily?) buys you some extra to spend on the important things in life.

And finally, if all else fails, lie. Swear blind that you've already done it, or that someone else is doing it—anything. This course will give you, as it has thousands of my satisfied students, the confidence to pull off some truly monstrous untruths with nobody daring to call your bluff. Believe me. Would I lie to you?

PRINCIPLE V INACTION

The underlying ground rules for avoiding extraneous exertion are few and simple, but often forgotten. In their most basic form they are:

➤ NEVER, EVER, VOLUNTEER FOR ANYTHING.

➤ DEADLINES ARE JUST GUIDELINES, AND ARE THERE TO BE IGNORED.

➤ THE THREE PS—POSTPONE, PROCRASTINATE, AND PREVARICATE.

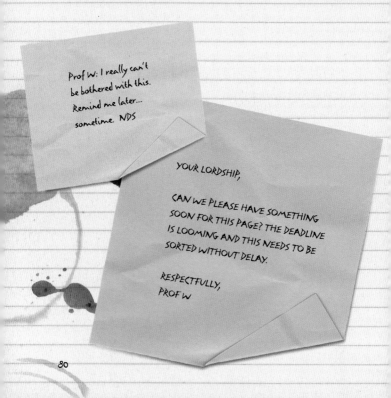

Prof W: I really can't be bothered with this. Remind me later... sometime. NDS

YOUR LORDSHIP,

CAN WE PLEASE HAVE SOMETHING SOON FOR THIS PAGE? THE DEADLINE IS LOOMING AND THIS NEEDS TO BE SORTED WITHOUT DELAY.

RESPECTFULLY,
PROF W

USEFUL DELAYING TECHNIQUES

Postponement	1. Flag *everything* "for future discussion" 2. Pass on as much as possible to colleagues for approval before action 3. Appear to be too busy to deal with things just at the moment
Procrastination	1. Displacement activity—find something else that demands your immediate attention (coffee, lunch, bathroom break, and so on) 2. Constantly reorganize your diary so that the immediate future is always free 3. Re-label in and out trays as "IN" and "Pre-IN"
Prevarication	1. When put on the spot, change the subject 2. Complicate simple tasks to buy yourself more time—blind them with science to avoid being specific 3. Have a ready list of excuses, scapegoats, and plausible lies

RISK? JUST SAY NO

Many of the sad losers who come to me for advice are really looking for some excitement to spice up their tedious lives. Well, if you want thrills and spills, take up whitewater rafting or something, don't bother me. The really Powerful People know that taking risks is an unnecessary business, and it saps energy that could be spent on more pleasurable pursuits. Take a tip from me: minimize any risk-taking, or there'll be Hell to pay.

Of course, you can't always avoid some element of risk; but if you have to take a gamble, use someone else's money. There's always somebody willing to part with their cash if you pitch it right. If all goes well, you get a good cut of the profit; if it bombs, it's their money down the toilet. My loyal team of investment advisors, stockbrokers, and commodity dealers will attest to this. But do keep your backers informed of their losses—they like to know—or you could end up being scapegoated (see page 115 for a case study of Nick Leeson). It's also a good idea to draw up a watertight contract with plenty of escape clauses in the fine print (I always insist on this. The Devil's in the detail).

One last thing: if you're working on commission, make sure the project's a biggie. Think about it... if you get, say, 10% commission, it's better to be selling private jets at $1m (commission $100,000 per unit sold) than boxes of matches at 10c (1c per unit). You have to sell a helluva lot of matches to earn the same as selling just one airplane.

PRINCIPLE VI IN ACTION

It's better to be a bookie than a bettor. Examine the odds, and do the math:

Take a three-horse race. Horse A has a pretty good track record, and looks like winning quite easily—let's say a 70% chance of coming in first. Horse B is a tired old nag, but could still surprise us, and has maybe a 20% chance of beating the other two. Horse C, on the other hand, is an out-and-out loser, only once coming in the first three; let's be generous and give her a 10% chance. (The chances add up to 100%.) So, the actual odds on the three horses are:

A: 3–7 (30–70)   B: 4–1 (80–20)   C: 9–1 (90–10)

But that's not what you, the bookie, offer. Oh no. You increase the percentages so A has an 80% chance, B a 30% chance, and C a 20% chance. So you offer odds like this:

A: 1–4 (20–80)   B: 7–3 (70–30)   C: 4–1 (80–20)

If you look carefully, you'll notice that the chances add up to 130% in this arrangement. And take it from me, that's not bad for you: if you accept bets in the correct proportions, for every $130 you take from the poor saps betting, you only pay back $100—whichever order the horses stumble across the finishing line.

Outlay—nix   Profit—30%

They're the sort of odds I like.

THE SIX PRINCIPLES OF SLOTH IN A NUTSHELL

666

i   All work and no play makes Jack a dumbass

ii   Why keep a dog and bark yourself?

iii   Take the credit

iv   Shift the blame

v   Never put off till tomorrow what you can do the day after

vi   Heads you win, tails they lose

WRATH

Management gurus and life coaches place a whole heap of emphasis on "people skills"—which in the business world refers to "human resources" (I just love that phrase! Describes my business to a T) and in social and family terms is all about "interpersonal relationships." Well, I'd agree that this is a crucially important area, but when they go on about empathy, understanding, and compromise, I know they've got the wrong end of the schtick.

All that touchy-feely baloney won't get you anywhere worth going. For too long we've been fed that corny "the meek shall inherit the earth" line by Mr. High-and-Mighty. Talk about double standards! If He thinks Wrath is such a sin (and what the hell's wrong with that anyway?), how come He played that hand so much in the Old Testament?

And my idea of anger management is totally different from theirs. To be up there with the Powerful People, you need to exercise your Wrath. Aggression is a basic instinct, after all: someone wants what you've got, you defend it; someone's got what you want, you attack. Trying to control Wrath is counterproductive—better, as we shall see in the following section, to unleash its power to control others. They won't like it, but they'll show you some respect.

"It's better to be feared than loved"

Principle i

NEVER GIVE A SUCKER
AN EVEN BREAK

To be effective as a means of control, Wrath must be made manifest.
That is, it's no good just being angry—you have to show you're angry.
Snarl, snap, and explode at the least provocation, and aim your ire
where it will hurt most.

This is a time-honored way of maintaining control. If you want to
exercise your power over someone (and who doesn't?), look for the
chink in their armor and go for it. Nip any signs of opposition or
incompetence in the bud with displays of rage, and they'll soon fall into
line. Dammit, some of them actually enjoy being ostracized. (see Section
II, Principle iii).

Just how far you let your anger go depends on the resilience of your
opponent: it can be anything from a mere threat through minor acts of
aggression such as a takeover, to dirty tricks like industrial espionage,
sabotage, blackmail, hitmen... the sky's the limit. Most satisfying of all,
it's true that the bigger they come, the harder they fall.

THE LESSON TO
BE LEARNED

Let them know
who's boss.

Happy
Valentine Nic
Love Al.

CASE STUDY: AL CAPONE

In the 1920s, Alphonse Capone had a good thing going in Chicago: speakeasies, moonshine, protection rackets—he turned out to be a model student. Unfortunately, another of my alumni, "Bugs" Moran, had ambitions in the same business sector. Negotiations between the two inevitably proved fruitless, so Capone's advisors "Greasy Thumb" Gusik and "The Enforcer" Nitti suggested a show of his displeasure. He got "Machine Gun" McGurn to assemble a team of hitmen, and on Valentine's Day 1929, disguised as policemen, they lured Moran's senior employees to a garage and mowed them down. Moran, as always, was late for the meeting and missed Capone's demonstration of Wrath, but he got the message and almost immediately went out of business.

Dear Bugsy

Love You

Al

PRINCIPLE I IN ACTION

Although I don't advocate holding on to your Wrath, or worse still, trying to control its effects, I do recommend a little restraint to ensure it is aimed at the most advantageous target.

Whenever possible, allow your anger to build up just below the surface so that it can be accessed quickly. Locate the weak spot in your opponent's defenses, and then focus on a point of contention that will trigger its release. In this way, the main thrust of your rage will be directed appropriately—and any overspill will act as a warning to those in the vicinity.

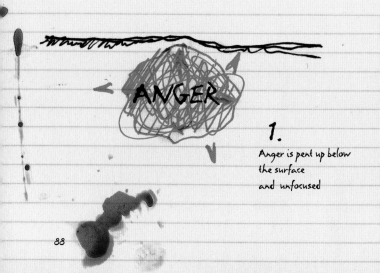

1.

Anger is pent up below the surface and unfocused

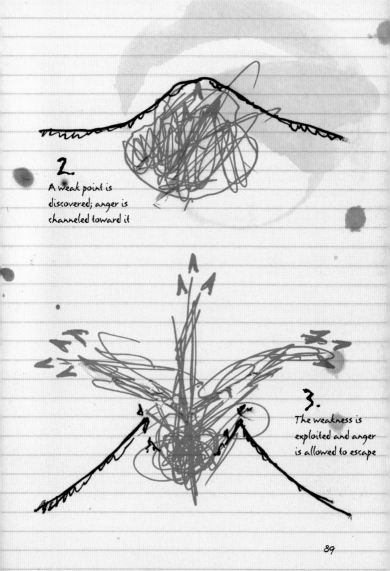

2.
A weak point is
discovered; anger is
channeled toward it

3.
The weakness is
exploited and anger
is allowed to escape

Principle ii

SCREW THEM
BEFORE THEY SCREW YOU

Now we have seen that Wrath can be an effective tool in personnel
management, let's examine how it can be most profitably employed.
The key here, as ever, is timing. Whenever possible, be one step ahead
of the competition, firing your ire at them before they have the chance
to get going.

If you can heap bile on potential opponents, you not only pull the mat
from under them by taking the wind out of their sails, and screwing up
their chances, but you also make an example of them to discourage any
future opposition.

At the first sign of any threat to your plans, get mad. Remember,

Anger is just Danger
    with its head removed.

CASE STUDY: JOSEPH McCARTHY

Although he was never one of my star pupils, Joe McCarthy had a real gift for accusation and smear campaigns. Anybody who even looked like they might be critical of his policies got the McCarthy treatment and ended up in front of HUAC (the House Committee on Un-American Activities —seems word-order wasn't a strong point), labeled as a communist or Soviet agent.

And to show that Hell hath no fury like a woman scorned, take a look at Margaret Thatcher: after only one consultation with me in the 1970s, she recognized the biggest threat to her holding power for a considerable time was the trade unions—so she introduced laws restricting and even eliminating organized labor. Attagirl!

THE LESSON TO BE LEARNED

Attack is the best form of defense.

And it's more fun, too.

PRINCIPLE II IN ACTION

The first, and crucial component is the element of surprise, catching your target off guard. This has the effect of stealing his thunder, which allows you to seize the initiative and remove all opposition, leaving the field open for you to reign supreme.

A useful way to look at this Principle is as a five-point gameplan:

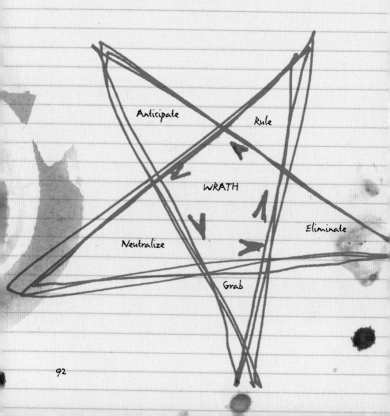

Anticipate	**S**tay alert for the slightest hint of competition or dissent, and plan to quash it before it can get started. Listen to the advice of those closest to you—but bear in mind it may be one of them.
Neutralize	**A**ct quickly to immobilize any threat. Use all methods at your disposal: discrediting and accusing opponents, blackmail, and counterthreats.
Grab	**T**his is the time to move in aggressively and take over, once you have weakened your opponents' defenses. Grab as many of their assets as possible, and encourage defectors.
Eliminate	**A**s the competition is now emasculated and their power base removed, it's relatively simple to clean up and get rid of all traces. Their supporters will just disappear, or come round to your side.
Rule	**N**ow that your opponents are out of the way, you can sit back and enjoy exercising the power. Further opposition is unlikely, since you have shown how you deal with dissent.

REVENGE IS A DISH BEST SERVED COLD

Sometimes a setback is unavoidable; once or twice, even I have missed the telltale signs of dissent and ended up with egg on my face. And of course, the natural reaction is rage—but don't get mad, get even. The really Powerful Person isn't tempted to lose his/her cool. Not yet.

A kneejerk reaction may give you immediate satisfaction, but it's likely to be short-lived, and just make you look like a sore loser. Rather than a sudden outburst, I recommend a "slow burn"

1. Focus	2. Delay
3. Trigger	4. Object
Signal	Opposition

technique in these circumstances. Take your time to build up a good head of steam, lulling your opponent into a false sense of security, and choose the moment to get your own payback. But don't leave it too long—there's no sense in being a damn fool about it.

PRINCIPLE III IN ACTION

Take time to prepare the components of your revenge: focusing your Wrath appropriately, determining a timescale, deciding an activation stimulus, and identifying the recipient. Only then can they be organized into a coherent sequence for optimum effect.

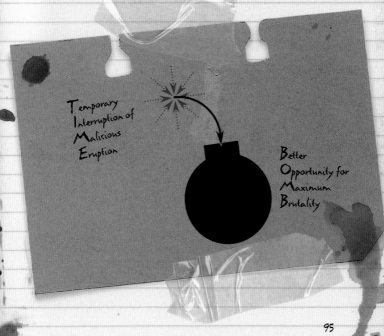

Temporary Interruption of Malicious Eruption

Better Opportunity for Maximum Brutality

Principle iv

HARVEST THE GRAPES OF WRATH

Just what do you achieve by venting your Wrath, apart from a warm glow of satisfaction? Well, a number of things, actually. It's a mighty weapon against those who cross you, for a start, and a pretty good deterrent to anybody thinking about it. More than that, your capacity for fury also establishes your place in the hierarchy, because a reputation for rage moves you further up the pecking order in any organization, and puts you at an advantage over your competitors.

Of course it goes without saying that the optimum position is at the top of the food chain, with nobody above you—and showing your aptitude for anger can help you get there.

It's fear that gives you the edge, and in my experience (which is long, and I dare anybody to contradict me) to keep the upper hand you have to maintain the level of threat. That involves not only regular (or even constant) shows of rage, but also letting everybody know that you've got something on them—even if you don't.

As you rise through the ranks, your displays of displeasure will become almost second nature. Don't let them become routine, however, or they will lose their potency: surprise is often a vital element. Besides, I always think unpredictability is just so much more fun.

PRINCIPLE IV IN ACTION

Establishing hierarchies (and ensuring your place at the top) is important not only in business but also in social and family situations. A well-organized structure is key to smooth operation, and needs to be maintained by strict discipline and a relentless monitoring of the threat—fear ratio.

The illustration opposite shows only a small selection of the ways in which you can enjoy exercising your Wrath while preserving or enhancing your status; as you progress, you will no doubt discover more of your own.

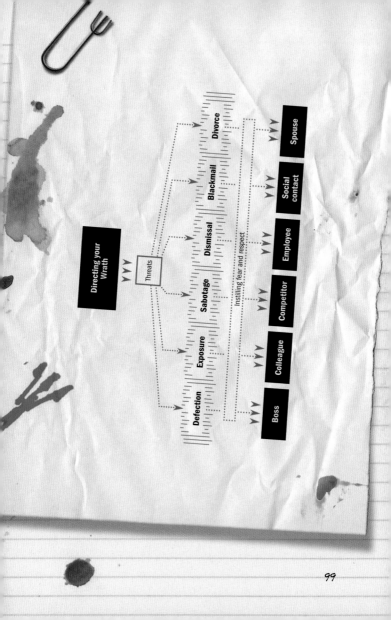

Directing your Wrath

Threats

Defection · Exposure · Sabotage · Dismissal · Blackmail · Divorce

Instilling fear and respect

Boss · Colleague · Competitor · Employee · Social contact · Spouse

Principle v

DON'T TEMPER YOUR TEMPER

It's not enough just to be angry, you have to really show you're angry—and in no uncertain terms. The thing is, you want your enemies and underlings to know, and remember, just how wrathful you are, otherwise you have to go through the wearisome business of asserting your authority time after time. So, make your displays of fury memorable. Mete out punishments, shout, threaten, bully, and blackmail. Go over the top, and give them both barrels. They'll love you for it. Well maybe not love you... but they'll know who's in charge.

THE LESSON TO BE LEARNED

When you blow your top, make sure you've got an appreciative audience.

CASE STUDY: NIKITA KHRUSHCHEV

If you need a role model for your Wrath, you don't need to look far.
Dictators through the ages (shows how long I've been in business)
have managed the transition from angry young man to vengeful old
SOB. Just have a look at some of their speeches some time: low on
rhetoric and reasoned policy, but right up there on fire and brimstone,
and they had their enemies—and their people—quaking in their boots.

Particularly fine displays of temper came from Adolf Hitler,
Augusto Pinochet, Saddam Hussein (especially when he punctuated
his speeches with gunfire), and Joe Stalin—but the prize goes to his
successor, Nikita Khrushchev, who during a debate at the UN took
off one of his shoes and banged it on the table. A great piece of
improvisation, Nik!

PRINCIPLE V IN ACTION

Wrath is not just about cussing and swearing, or raising your voice, pleasant though that might be. Oh no. There's a whole slew of different grades of Wrath, and a corresponding range of ways to express it. A good rule of thumb, I find, is to always go for one degree higher than the stimulus apparently deserves for maximum effect.

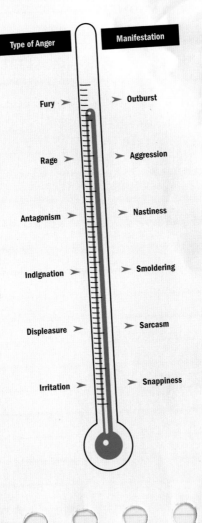

Principle vi

STICK TO YOUR GUNS

When the red mist descends, it's all too easy to lose sight of your objectives. As Wrath flies off the handle, reason flies out the window, and attempts to calm you down might tempt you to veer off your original course. Luckily, rage often has the effect of blinding its user to all but the object of his rage—and that's no bad thing.

You see, it doesn't matter whether you're right or wrong, it's just how forcibly you make your case. Opinions don't amount to a pile of crap—it's strong leadership that gains respect, so don't give in. The chariot of Wrath has no reverse gear, and is incapable of U-turns.

When in negotiations, don't concede anything. It will become a battle of wills, and there can only be one winner—make sure it's you by demonstrating your anger potential. Oh, and fight dirty.

CASE STUDY: IRAQ

I was put in a tricky situation around the turn of the millennium, with two of my students vying to see who could be the most Wrathful. If you'd asked me then, I'd have put my money on Goddam Hussein, but surprisingly young Bush came out on top in the end—he's not the sharpest tool in the box, but then he did have his pal Blair egging him on. Sure, Saddam could get pretty mad, but Georgie W. retaliated with ire of biblical proportions. Despite demonstrable evidence that Hussein had no WMDs and was not connected to Al Qaeda, he and Tony went in with guns blazing to exact retribution, and even found time to aim a few shots across the bows of Iran and North Korea too. Quite a shock for Saddam, but an awesome performance.

THE LESSON TO BE LEARNED

It isn't whether you're right or wrong, it's the amount of Wrath that wins in the end.

PRINCIPLE VI IN ACTION

It helps if you have a target for your wrath when fighting a battle.
Choose something that you know is likely to get you maximum support
(it really doesn't matter what it is—you're in this to win, not prove a
point). Find out exactly what is at the heart of your opposition, and
adopt an antithetical stance. Focus all your energy on this, then turn
your sights once again to your target, aiming for the very core—and
don't stray from this course until you hit home.

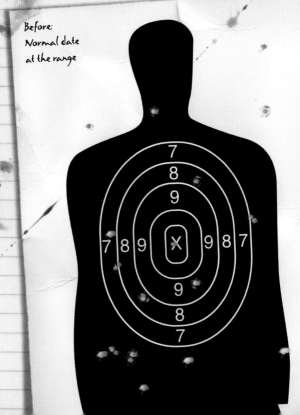

Before:
Normal date
at the range

After:
Wrath has
been harnessed
to achieve
objective

THE SIX PRINCIPLES OF WRATH IN A NUTSHELL

i   Accentuate the positive, eliminate the negative

ii   To err is human, to forgive is dumb

iii   Look back in Anger

iv   Let them know who's number one

v   Speak loudly, and carry a big stick

vi   Remember—compromise compromises

TRIDENT TESTED

ENVY

In an attempt to discourage use of this handy little self-improvement tool, some goody-goodies have referred to Envy as the "green-eyed monster"— an unwarranted slur, although I admit that Leviathan, the demon I've appointed to oversee Envy and all related operations, does have attractively bloodshot emerald eyes, and something of a weight problem.

But that's not the point. In very much the same way as Lust, Envy provides a potent motivating energy, and if handled in the right way can spur the user to greater things. What's more, as you make your way up the ladder, you can start playing on other people's envy too, just as you can exploit their Lust. In this way, Envy provides a means of control and power.

As well as giving you the motivation to emulate or surpass your rivals' achievements, Envy provides a stimulus to removing the competition. When it comes in the form of simple jealousy (i.e., someone's got what you think by rights should be yours) it provokes an element of revenge: instead of matching your competitors' assets, you actually take them for yourself, killing two birds with one stone.

"I'll have what he's having"

Principle i

LOOK AROUND AND SEE WHAT YOU'RE MISSING

At first sight, Envy would seem to be easy to recognize and utilize—it's what you feel when you see someone having a good time and you want some too. Well, true—but you might be missing something. Far better to keep your eyes open and scout about specifically for things to covet. You'll then find there's a lot more than you thought, and some of it much better than you ever dreamed of.

Time for another analogy: A guy riding a bicycle notices his friend driving a little Japanese car. He wants one too. Error! He should have stopped and wondered what his friend was envying, and had a look at what else was on the road. Then he would target his envy on the owner of the chauffeur-driven limousine.

The message is this: raise your sights and aim for the top. Even when you've got the limo, don't stop looking—the next guy's got an executive jet. And so on, ad infinitum.

DOING GOD'S WORK? OH, C'MON ...

CASE STUDY: TELEVANGELISTS

Following the success of that dreadful loudmouth Bill Graham (he really let me down, the double-crossing do-gooder), there was a spate of evangelical preachers anxious to emulate the fame and fortune shtick he pulled off. My contracts department was positively overwhelmed by requests for assistance in conning the happy-clappies out of large sums of cash. Luckily the time was right for using the new technology, and a number of the televangelists did very well out of it—Oral Roberts's hysterical pleas and threats of divine retribution (nice touch!) were particularly successful. But some were carried away by the "love thy neighbor" bit. It was a joy to see my former acolytes Jimmy Swaggart and Jim Bakker trade accusations of fornication with one another in the fight for a congregation. Turned out they were both guilty as hell, as I could have told you when they signed on the dotted line.

PRINCIPLE 1 IN ACTION

A straightforward example showing how improvement achieved
in purely monetary terms can be used as a model for any kind of
self-promotion through Envy.

A base of inadequate or even negative resources creates a need which is
augmented by Greed. Rather than simply satisfy this in a haphazard
way, the shrewd operator will examine the situation to see if he can
discover an existing solution which is worthy of his Envy, before letting
this provide the power for securing an adequate means of acquisition.

In other words, when you're desperate, take a bit of time to look around
and see what you can grab that will take you to the top.

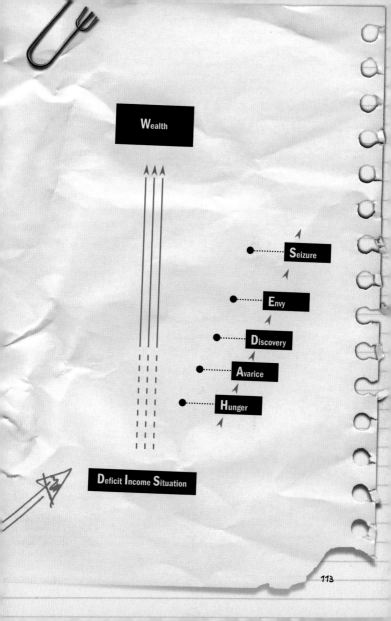

Principle ii

I WANT A PIECE
OF THE ACTION!

As you look around and see what you're missing out on, think about different ways that you can get in on the act. It's not always possible to take over or steal someone else's gravy train, so you have to find a way of worming your way in and taking what you can from the inside.

It might be a question of working for someone (preferably on commission)—or better, persuading them to let you work your own scam using their assets. There are all kinds of good con opportunities about these days, as the global free-market economy is just crying out to be exploited. Blind your investors (while robbing them blind) with mumbo jumbo pretending to offer a new economic paradigm. You can even get away with old tricks like cooking the books or loan sharking if you give them fancy names like "creative accounting" or "sub-prime lending." You can also turn a profit in a falling market by "short-selling": just borrow stock, sell it, and wait for the price to drop before buying it back cheap and pocketing the difference. If all goes well, nobody will never notice.

CASE STUDY: HIGH FINANCE

Sometimes, one of my high-flying students goes on to do really well for himself by taking the lessons he learned to a new level. One such was Alan Greenspan, Chairman of the US Federal Reserve from 1987 to 2006. He advocated deregulation of just about every financial institution in the name of the free market, allowing all sorts of marvelous malpractices. Cleverly (actually, on my advice) he got out and found a nice little retirement job just before the shit hit the fan, passing the mantle on to Ben Bernanke—who, it has to be said, was just as ingenious when it came to protecting the fat cats. When the banks went belly up in 2008, Bernanke, with US Treasury Secretary Hank Paulson (two of my best students) managed to screw over $700 billion out of the state coffers, creating a precedent that established the admirable principle: The banks get to keep any profit, and the taxpayer covers any loss. Brilliant.

THE LESSON TO BE LEARNED

Don't be afraid to gamble with borrowed money. Just make sure you cover your ass first.

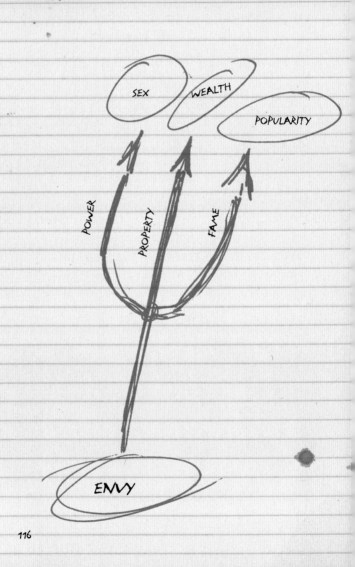

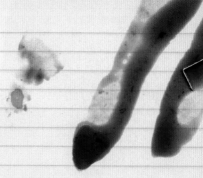

PRINCIPLE II IN ACTION

Envy is closely related to Lust, and (as we shall see in the following pages) has many similar properties. The objects of Envy are in fact the same as those that provoke Lust: Wealth and Property, Sex and Power, and Popularity and Fame.

As with so many things in life, one thing leads to another. Envy, your core motivation in this scenario, may be triggered by any one of a whole raft of desirables, but inevitably prompts a tripartite progression which incorporates multiple goals.

Allowing your Envy to work simultaneously on three different levels will not diminish its potency: on the contrary, in fact, because they are working in the same direction. The trick here is to find the appropriate means to spearhead your assault on those goals. By getting a foot in the door of the object of your Envy, you can tap in to his or her Power, Property, and Fame and use this to acquire yet more, and subsequently spur you to nailing the Sex, Wealth, and Popularity you've been craving.

PRINCIPLE III: WHO ATE MY CHEESE?

It helps if you can personalize your Envy. Instead of vaguely longing for abstract ideals, pin them down to people who have the lifestyle you aspire to. Instead of saying "I want Wealth (or Power, or Fame, or whatever)," say "I want to be Wealthy (or Famous, or Powerful), like X."

In this way you can visualize your goals more easily, and build up a healthy resentment. It also makes it easier to see what strategies to use (Greed, Lust, Sloth, or Wrath, for example)— and see how the object of your Envy has done it. Then beat him at his own game. That's the payoff that makes quenching your Envy so gratifying.

PRINCIPLE III IN ACTION

Envy can pull you in many directions at once. Don't let this worry you—the more you Envy in any one direction, the more it's likely to lead to Envy in other areas too. If you are jealous of someone's Wealth, you'll soon be envious of his Power and Popularity. This helps to increase the scope of your actions, so there's no reason why you should restrict yourself to any one aspiration.

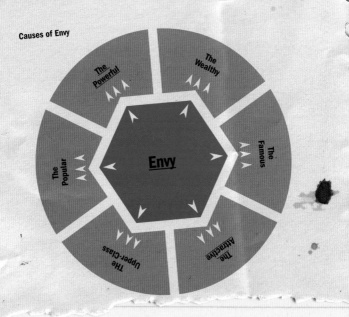

Causes of Envy

The Powerful · The Wealthy · The Famous · The Attractive · The Upper-Class · The Popular · **Envy**

LOCATE THE SELFISH GENE

It's taken a long time for science to discover the freaking obvious. Darwin nearly got it when I told him about the survival of the tightfisted, but I think he misheard. It wasn't until the 20th century that some geneticist realized progress is a result of selfishness. I ask you—do you really need a PhD to come up with that?

Ah well, at least they're confirming what I knew all along: being selfish is an essential part of the Powerful Person's makeup. If you want to get ahead, you've got to know what you want, and Envy plays a large part in that—but to stay ahead, you've got to know how to keep it.

Getting in touch with your Envy is a major step towards realizing a fundamental truth: the road to success is built on a foundation of egoism. When you see what arouses your Greed and Lust, Envy is the trigger—but it's selfishness that pulls it.

It's such a fundamental principle (underlying every other principle in this book), that it often gets overlooked. So let me put it plainly and simply—look out for number one. Me, me, me. Satisfy all your envious cravings, while at the same time jealously guarding what you've got.

In business, that means squeezing out or buying up the competition and creating a monopoly so that nobody gets a shot, but the principle holds good in other areas of life too. Whatever the situation, the rule is: take what you envy, but hold onto what is envied.

120

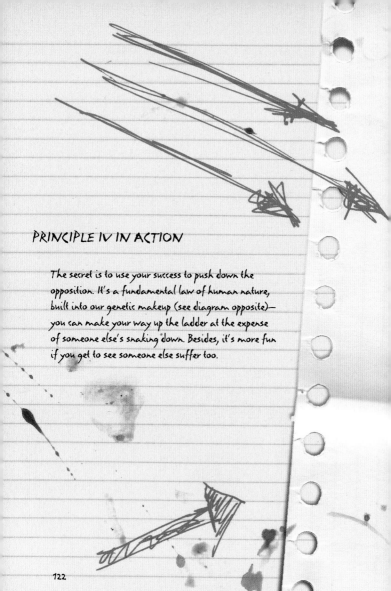

PRINCIPLE IV IN ACTION

The secret is to use your success to push down the
opposition. It's a fundamental law of human nature,
built into our genetic makeup (see diagram opposite)—
you can make your way up the ladder at the expense
of someone else's snaking down. Besides, it's more fun
if you get to see someone else suffer too.

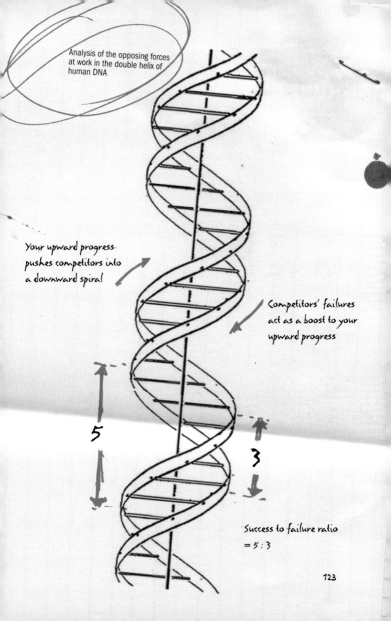

Analysis of the opposing forces at work in the double helix of human DNA

Your upward progress pushes competitors into a downward spiral

Competitors' failures act as a boost to your upward progress

5

3

Success to failure ratio = 5 : 3

Principle v

IF IT'S GOOD ENOUGH FOR HIM, IT'S EVEN BETTER FOR ME

One of the nicest things about Envy is what it teaches us about other people. Once you recognize that you deserve X, Y, or Z as much as the other guy, you begin to realize that you'd actually appreciate it more than he does. Ergo, it's wasted on him.

This gives you if not exactly the moral high ground (and let's face it, do you really need the moral high ground?), then at least an inherent right to what he's got by virtue of your innate superiority. He may not see it that way though, and will try to regain his advantage, starting the ball rolling in a game of leapfrog which mushrooms to everybody's benefit.

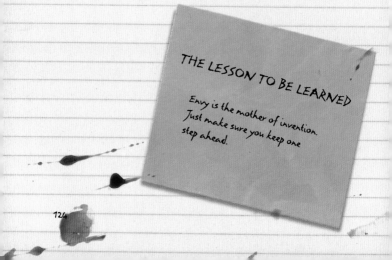

THE LESSON TO BE LEARNED

Envy is the mother of invention. Just make sure you keep one step ahead.

CASE STUDY: THE ARMS RACE

The Arms Race started with the invention of the very first weapon (a large rock, hurled at a rival caveman. I know, because I was there egging them on), and culminated in the aptly acronymed Mutually Assured Destruction of the nuclear-fueled Cold War. The rules of the game are simplicity itself: Player A threatens player B with a weapon; B retaliates by threatening with a bigger, better weapon. Each is bargaining on the Envy of the other, and thus upping the ante. A subsidiary play is to encourage a minor conflict on the fringes of the area of play, justifying further defense budget increases. Each increase in offensive power provides an excuse for another, and everybody's happy. Especially the arms dealers.

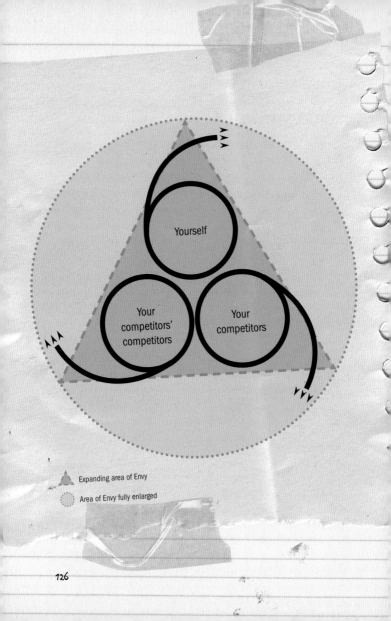

Yourself

Your competitors' competitors

Your competitors

Expanding area of Envy

Area of Envy fully enlarged

PRINCIPLE V IN ACTION

As your Envy increases, it pushes the boundaries of what can be achieved. That goes for the Envy of your competitors and their competitors too, as they strive to keep up with one another. The net effect is to create a perpetual motion that keeps the cycle of production—consumption turning.

In economic terms, it's this cycle that ensures the system carries on growing—and economic growth is what it's all about. Envy incentivizes the urge to create wealth. Sure, there may be a few losers along the way, but don't be seduced by the bleeding hearts and their theories of sustainable development, zero-growth economies, and (worse still) equitable redistribution. It's a jungle out there in the real world, and in the dog-eat-dog rat race, it's every man for himself.

Principle vi

I LIKED IT SO MUCH,
I BOUGHT THE COMPANY

Think of Envy like an itch. It's not really a pleasant sensation per se, the
enjoyment comes when you try to get rid of it. With an itch, the pleasure
is in the scratching; with Envy, the gratification comes from acquiring
—or better still, taking. Equaling the success of the object of your Envy is a
joy, but if you snatch it from him it's a double whammy. Bliss.

There are basically three degrees of Envy satisfaction,
best illustrated thus:

See a product that sells? *Copy it.*

See an idea that's got potential? *Steal it.*

See a company that's doing well? *Buy it.*

Or even more simply:

Take

Take away

Take over

It's not difficult to see how all three examples will
satisfy your Envy, but the third has the added advantage
of removing the competition. No contest.

128

CASE STUDY: VICTOR KIAM

A consummate salesman, Victor Kiam made his fortune from other people's ideas and became famous for telling the world how he did it in a series of 1980s TV commercials. Chutzpah or what? The story, for those who don't know, is that his wife bought him a Remington shaver that he liked so much, you guessed it, he bought the company. But the stroke of genius (for which he takes all the credit, but was actually my idea) was to use the story as the punchline in advertising the product. It seems he liked quite a lot of products, as he went on to buy up other companies too. In fact, he acquired businesses like most people buy... well, razors. It's a cutthroat world out there.

THE LESSON TO BE LEARNED

Act on your Envy, and you'll be the Envy of your competitors.

NEW!

The Sensational REMINGTON 60 ELECTRIC DRY SHAVER

For the first time in shaving history the sixty second shave is possible. You may not want to shave that fast, but 50 men, under supervision, tried for ten days with the new Remington 60 and averaged 54 seconds a shave. The two new, extra long shaving heads are mounted on the live Remington Contour principle, slightly arched to fit easily into hard-to-shave spots. Regular Model 210-250v. AC/DC. Dual Volt 110-150 and 190-250v. AC/DC.

The Perfectionist. Ask for Remington Pre-Shave and After-Shave Lotions and Powder Stick.

The Sixty Second Shaving Marvel!

Remington Rand Ltd., 1-19 New Oxford Street, W.C.1

129

PRINCIPLE VI IN ACTION

Envy emanates from the area we shall call the Circle of Interest, which acts outward, seeking new goals. Within this is the Circle of Influence, which deals with affairs over which it already has some control. When Envy has selected its target, the Circle of Interest is drawn toward it, with the aim of bringing it into the Circle of Influence.

In practical terms, the four stages in a successful takeover are:

➤ Make your Circle of Interest exceed your Circle of Influence at all times, and be constantly on the lookout for things to Envy

➤ When you see a suitable candidate, let your Envy drive you to take a greater interest

➤ Now make this your primary area of interest and make moves toward gaining some control

➤ When the time is right, swallow up the entire concern, satisfying your Envy and removing a rival from the field

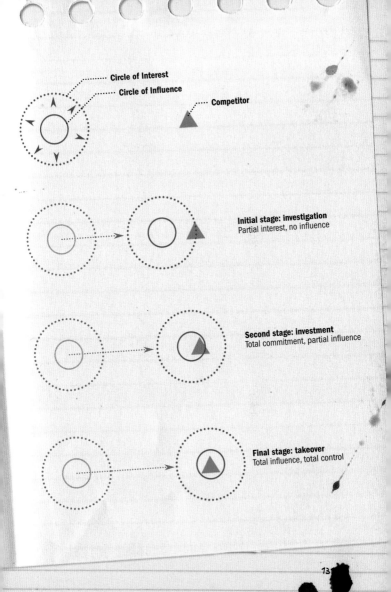

Circle of Interest

Circle of Influence

Competitor

Initial stage: investigation
Partial interest, no influence

Second stage: investment
Total commitment, partial influence

Final stage: takeover
Total influence, total control

73

THE SIX PRINCIPLES OF ENVY IN A NUTSHELL

i   The grass actually is greener on the other side

ii You can't have your cake and eat it—so take somebody else's piece

iii Make it personal

iv Don't take it easy. Take it. Easy!

v   It's not keeping up with the Joneses, it's staying ahead of the game

vi The customer is always right (but only when you're doing the buying)

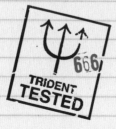

PRIDE

Following on from the heels, Envy, we now come to its complement—Pride—as we round off our course in self-improvement with a few lessons on self-promotion. Where Envy motivates you to do something, Pride tells the world what you've done. As well as helping you to make your way to the top, Pride has the added bonus of being an aid to holding on to the Power that you have gained along the way.

Just as a craftsman takes Pride in his work, we should all be proud of our achievements, if only to rub salt into the wounds of those we've defeated in the process. As we shall see, Pride comes in several guises (I rely on Lucifer to light the way in these matters—he positively glows with self-satisfaction), and can be put to as many uses, but is particularly relevant to the student who has successfully put into practice the principles laid down in this book.

A brilliant idea, if I do say so myself.

"If you've got it, flaunt it"

THE PRIDE OF LIONS

If you've been taking my advice so far, you will be finding yourself among the Powerful People, the Rich and Famous. Time to sit back and enjoy, you might think—but why not go the extra mile and really make the most of it? You could even enhance your position or at the very least make it more secure.

Yes, we're talking Pride here: publicizing your achievements and letting everybody know how successful you are. You can capitalize on your success to take you even farther, by continually sending out the message: "I am a successful person." Even if you're not.

THE LESSON TO BE LEARNED

Publicizing your success will make you more successful, and your fame will make you more famous. And you can get rich quick selling advice on how to get rich quick.

CASE STUDY: SELF-HELP GURUS

Remember Charles Atlas, the muscleman who promised "You too can have a body like mine"? By advertising what he was proud of, he became world-famous—but also tapped into the average sucker's deep desire to be better and made a fortune. These days the macho image doesn't sell so well, but success in business, or in life generally, does.

There is no end to the series of self-help courses available, all saying the same thing: "You too can have success like mine." And, like Charles Atlas, life coaches such as Dale Carnegie, Stephen R. Covey, Thomas J. Peters, and Deepak Chopra (I could go on. And on) have achieved fame and fortune by telling the world how they achieved fame and fortune. Most of it is hooey, of course, and nothing you didn't already know, but the more the ideas sell, the more respected the guru becomes—and the more he benefits from his Pride.

PRINCIPLE I IN ACTION

Much depends how you look at the situation—and how you present yourself. Interpretation of the situation is all-important, as is an optimistic evaluation of your achievements. There are multiple ways to perspectivize any scenario, but only one correct interpretation that can maximize expectations for an optimal result.

As an example, let's look at an apparently straightforward and unambiguous symbol, the number 6. Looked at from another angle, it can be seen as a 9 (a potentially dangerous misinterpretation).

To extend this example, rotation of the character (using three views of the number 6) provides us with a useful graphical mnemonic (see diagrams opposite).

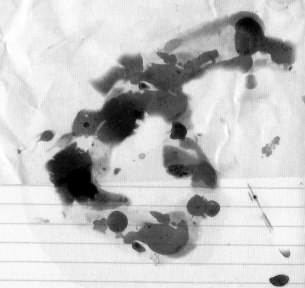

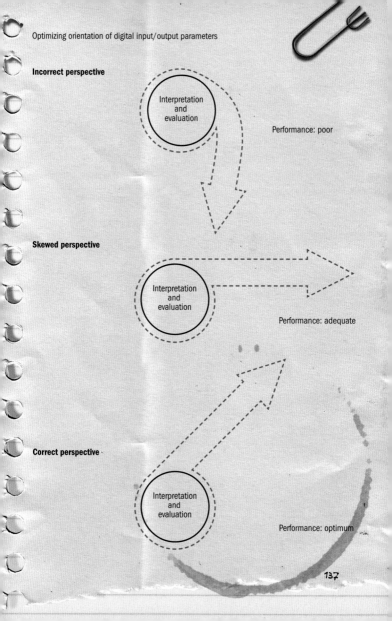

Incorrect perspective

Interpretation and evaluation

Performance: poor

Skewed perspective

Interpretation and evaluation

Performance: adequate

Correct perspective

Interpretation and evaluation

Performance: optimum

137

Principle ii

LOOK DOWN ON THOSE WHO LOOK UP TO YOU

On your way up, one of the tools you use is Envy, which has you looking up to those who have got what you want; Pride is the flip side of the coin, showing you how to make sure those envying you don't get in on the act. And, most satisfyingly, how to look down on them with disdain. This affects the way you interact with them, and makes it easier for you to use them mercilessly.

Conventional wisdom dictates that you should show respect to those you meet on the way up, because you may meet them again on the way down. I treat that idea with the contempt it deserves—my advice is to treat your rivals (and customers) with the contempt they deserve too. Learn to tread all over them and they'll act as stepping stones. And who ever heard of a stepping stone biting back?

PRINCIPLE II IN ACTION

At every step on the ladder to the top, it's vital that you make your position unassailable. At the lowest level, your Envy is your strongest weapon, but once you have reached a median position Pride must take its place. Pride in your achievements shows your strength and deters any attack from those that envy you. Once at the top, Pride becomes your Primary Power, and to maintain superiority it must always exceed the strength of their Envy. In this way, a pecking order is established, and everybody knows their place.

← Direction of Envy
→ Direction of Pride

Position of Pride   Median Position   Position of Envy

BE PROUD TO BE PROUD

I spend much of the time with my clients undoing the harm done by do-gooders, pointing out the error of "virtues" like hard work, tolerance, and abstinence. Perhaps the worst of their misconceptions is modesty—but then, they've got plenty to be modest about.

No, modesty—even false modesty—spells disaster. You've got to keep telling everybody how wonderful you are. The more you say it, the more they'll believe you, and the better you'll do. When it comes to publicity, there's no such thing as failure: if you've had setbacks, tell them your hard luck story, and how you've managed to succeed against insurmountable odds. The main thing is to be relentless in your pursuit of self-promotion, because the moment you let up, someone else will steal the limelight.

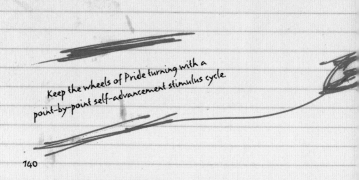

Keep the wheels of Pride turning with a point-by-point self-advancement stimulus cycle.

PRINCIPLE III IN ACTION

Forget all that "Pride comes before a fall" crap—Pride should be right there at the heart of any venture. It's not just about selling yourself and your products and services; there's a whole bundle of useful kickbacks that interact to form a self-perpetuating cycle of advancement.

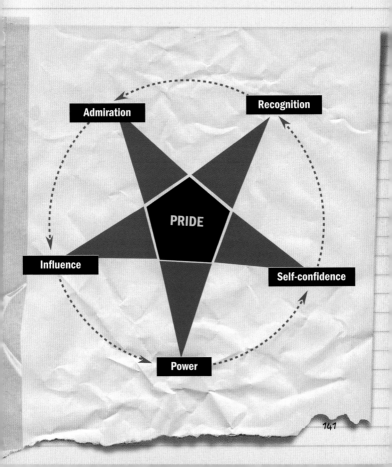

Principle iv

WEAR YOUR HEART ON YOUR SLEEVE, ALONGSIDE THE SCALPS ON YOUR BELT

Don't be a shrinking violet when it comes to Pride. Pull out all the stops and give it to them with both barrels—you have to play to the gallery and give them what they want to hear. That means boasting, bragging, exaggerating, and embroidering your story, and using every rhetorical trick in the book to hype up your reputation.

Play on their emotions, tug at their heartstrings, and get them on your side. Tell them not only how difficult it was (but you managed, obviously), but also who you had to defeat along the way. You'll get their sympathy, and ultimately their respect. Then you can get away with murder.

Sympathy for the Devil

CASE STUDY: RICHARD NIXON

I've always had a soft spot for Tricky Dicky, because he had a natural ability to look as if butter wouldn't melt in his mouth while he was lying through his teeth. His facility for bragging about his credentials got him reelected as Vice President and President of the US (okay, I pulled a few strings too), and even when faced with impeachment he kept saying how great he was and had done nothing wrong—just "errors of judgement." Sadly, Watergate was his Waterloo, but he managed to make even that a triumph with the tearful rhetoric of his resignation speech. Bravo, Dick, and welcome to my team.

THE LESSON TO BE LEARNED

The most important thing is sincerity. Once you can fake that, you've got it made.

SPOT THE DIFFERENCE

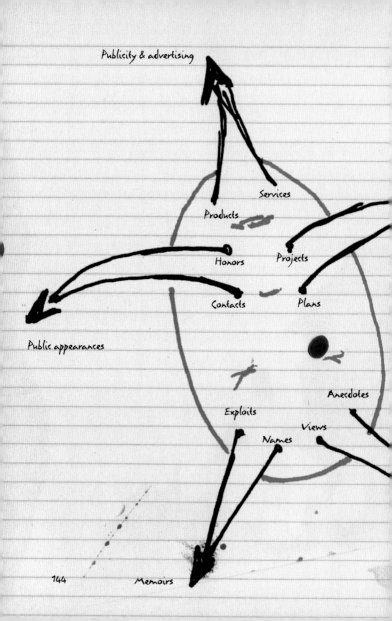

Publicity & advertising

Services

Products

Honors

Projects

Public appearances

Contacts

Plans

Anecdotes

Exploits

Views

Names

144

Memoirs

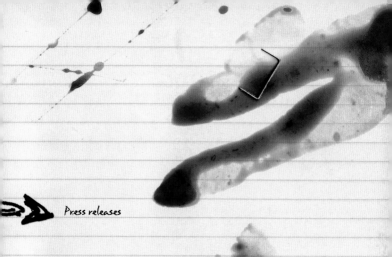

 Press releases

PRINCIPLE IV IN ACTION

When promoting yourself, choose the medium carefully to maximize the effect, but above all make the most of every opportunity. This may entail putting out information in several different directions at once, as can be seen in the diagram opposite. Failure to explore every avenue could result in overturning the entire structure, and disaster will be staring you in the face.

Interviews

Principle v

NOBODY LOVES A LOSER

So now you know that Pride will keep you on the up and up, and that hyping your success will accelerate your rise. You've also seen how it helps to show the competition you met along the way. Well, you'll look a whole lot better if you can provide some good (or rather bad) comparisons too.

For every one of your triumphs, highlight your achievement by showing someone else's failure. Badmouthing the opposition—especially when they've screwed up—puts your position into context, and the contrast makes your Pride really glow. So, point out all the losers who failed where you have succeeded. What's more, it provides an opportunity to learn from their mistakes—you don't want to end up like them, do you?

THE LESSON TO BE LEARNED

Don't be a sore loser. Find some way of bringing others down with you, and ending up on top.

Great sense of timing, Ken!

CASE STUDY: KENNETH LAY

The mastermind behind what was then the biggest bankruptcy
in US history, Kenneth Lay, could so easily have ended up as just
another sad loser. But his Pride, in the form of insistence that he
was innocent, carried him through. When his fraud and corruption
came to light, it brought down the Enron corporation and all those
associated with its financial dealings, and Lay was convicted on
11 counts of fraud—but pulled off a magnificent stroke by dying
before he was sentenced. His conviction was abated by a federal
appellate court (in other words, he got off scot-free and his estate
was left intact), and he came out of the affair a winner. Okay, only
posthumously, but it did land him a permanent (very permanent) job
as a consultant accountant with me.

PRINCIPLE V IN ACTION

It's important to be aware of the dangers associated with being
in a position of prominence. Pride, and its manifestation, must be
maintained at the highest possible levels at all times to avoid the risk of
a fall from grace. I suffered a similar descent very early in my career,
and it was an instructive experience.

The telltale signs often come in the form of a loss of confidence,
which your rivals will inevitably seize upon. Unless this is nipped in the
bud, doubt about your abilities as a Powerful Person will creep in, and
the downward spiral is already out of your control. The struggle to
maintain your position, let alone attempt a comeback, depletes your
resources and defeat is unavoidable. As you approach the bottom, you
face a Defeated Inferiority Situation—abandon hope, all you who enter
here. You have been warned.

Descent from Dominance through the circles of Hostile Evaluation of Leadership Liabilities

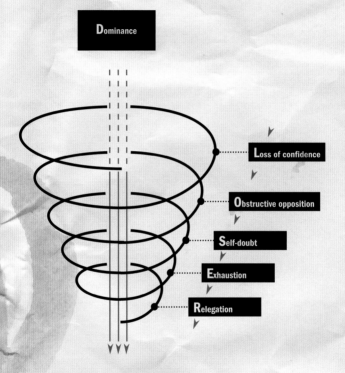

Dominance

Loss of confidence

Obstructive opposition

Self-doubt

Exhaustion

Relegation

Defeated Inferiority Situation

EVER WONDER WHY EVERYBODY'S HEARD OF THE RICHEST MAN IN BABYLON?

One of the so-called secrets of the Rich and Famous (and it's interesting how often those two adjectives are seen side by side) is that they are rich because they're famous, and famous because they're rich.

Even the reclusive hermits of the billionaire set make sure everybody knows how wealthy they are. Look at the Forbes 100 list; no shrinking violets there. Even if you don't make it to the rich lists, make sure everybody knows how well you're doing—it doesn't matter if you aren't—and before you know it you'll be up there with them.

THE LESSON TO BE LEARNED:

Whenever possible, control the means of publicizing your success.

RICH FAMOUS

overnment why not jo

vovember has been anothe ficult month for the mo

CASE STUDY: RUPERT MURDOCH

Now here's a coincidence. One of the richest and most powerful men on the planet, Rupert Murdoch, made his fortune from the media. On the face of it, he's quite a reclusive guy, keeping his private life out of the limelight—but actually using his various media empires to publicize his success, making him a household name. Oh, and using his newspapers, TV stations, and satellite broadcasting to advertise... his satellite broadcasting, TV stations, and newspapers. Nifty.

Dear Nic,
Thanks for the gift.

PRINCIPLE VI IN ACTION

Pride, it almost goes without saying, increases fame. And fame gives more reason to be proud—the two are inextricably interlinked (see fig. i), and have a domino effect on one another.

But let's go one step farther: Fame and fortune go hand in hand too, and are thus dependent on the degree of Pride. Nobody got rich by being a nobody, and nobody got famous by being poor. It follows that Fame (Fa) is proportional to Fortune (Fo)—and, obviously, vice versa. In fact, Fame is proportional to Fortune in the ratio:

$$Fa : Fo^2$$

Popularity (P) plays a part in this equation too (see fig. ii) in that:

$$P = Fa \times \sqrt{Fo}$$

Where the initial level of Fame is determined by the Pride:Fame coordinates derived from fig. i.

Simple!

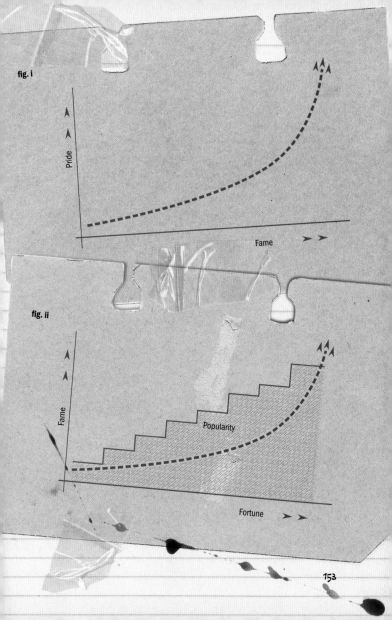

fig. i

Pride

Fame

fig. ii

Fame

Popularity

Fortune

THE SIX PRINCIPLES OF PRIDE IN A NUTSHELL

i   Don't be ashamed to blow your own trumpet

666

ii The view's best from the top of the tree

iii There's no such thing as bad publicity

iv Tell it like it is. Or like it should be

v   How are the mighty fallen

vi It pays to advertise

666

CHART YOUR PERSONAL PROGRESS
WITH THIS HANDY CHECKLIST

1   Have I acquired an appetite for success? ☐
2   Am I aiming to achieve my utmost potential? ☐
3   Do I make the most of advantageous opportunities? ☐
4   Am I only satisfied with the best? ☐
5   Will I do anything to turn a profit? ☐
6   Do I allow my success to spur me on? ☐
7   Am I in touch with my inner demon? ☐
8   Are my desires my core motivation? ☐
9   Do I truly enjoy my ruthlessness? ☐
10   Am I making the most of my charms? ☐
11   Have I learned the value of charisma? ☐
12   Is my libido channeled efficiently? ☐
13   Do I maintain a relaxed attitude to work-related issues? ☐
14   Have I mastered the art of task assignment? ☐
15   Am I at (or near) the top of any hierarchy? ☐
16   Do I have a complete disregard for culpability? ☐
17   Is my work–life balance satisfactory? ☐
18   Is risk aversion a priority in my decision-making? ☐
19   Am I prepared to lay down my friends for my life? ☐
20   Can I anticipate and pre-empt any hostility? ☐
21   Do I, when necessary, postpone retribution? ☐
22   Are my feelings made clear to those around me? ☐
23   Do I demonstrate an appropriate level of displeasure? ☐
24   Have I developed a killer instinct? ☐
25   Can I recognize opportunities for improvement? ☐
26   Am I effectively using all available resources? ☐
27   Can I visualize goal-oriented strategies? ☐
28   Do I put myself first? ☐
29   Can I see in others what could be good for me? ☐
30   Have I prioritized emulation, procurement, and acquisition? ☐
31   Do I make the most of my innate abilities? ☐
32   Am I adequately asserting my superiority? ☐
33   Am I making the most of promotion outlets? ☐
34   Is my self-marketing process fit for purpose? ☐
35   Is my self-esteem sufficiently high? ☐
36   Am I in total control of my fortune? ☐

If you can tick "yes" to all the above—congratulations! You're a success!

INDEX

ABOUT THE AUTHOR

Nicholas D. Satan was just another angel until he quit the firm—the firm Ament, that is—and got down to running his own business. That was way before the Fall (in which he played no small part), and since then he has built up a worldwide corporation whose clients include emperors, kings, presidents, and captains of industry.

How to Win Fiends and Influence People is a take-no-prisoners management and manipulation manual for home and office. Satan offers practical advice—based on the Seven Deadly Sins—to acquiring the diabolic habits necessary for dominance in life and in the workplace.

Lord Satan, author of *The Devil's Diaries* (Lyons Press), has offices in all major centers of power, and works from his base at Satancorp® HQ in the underworld city of Dis. He lives with his wife, children, and some goats in one of the quieter circles of Hell, and relaxes at his holiday homes in Haiti and Babylon.

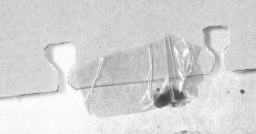

ACKNOWLEDGMENTS

I should like to thank the many academic, economic, and legal experts without whose help this book would not have seen the light of day; the editorial advice offered by the publishers, and in particular the solicitude of Ms. Lorraine Turner, has proved invaluable, and the skill of Herr Joerg Hartmannsgruber in restoring and deciphering very fragile documents has been at times revelatory.

The Dark Lord has also asked that I make mention of the many students of his methods, past and present, who have provided him with inspiration to persevere with the task of organizing this material into a coherent form for the edification of those prepared to read it with an open mind.

For my part, I must once again express my gratitude to His Satanic Majesty for granting me the honor of assisting him in this project.

Professor M. J. Weeks,
November 2008